⌂ SUCCESSFUL GARAGES AND CARPORTS

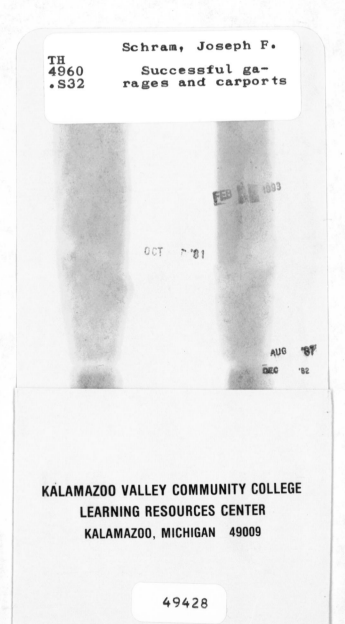

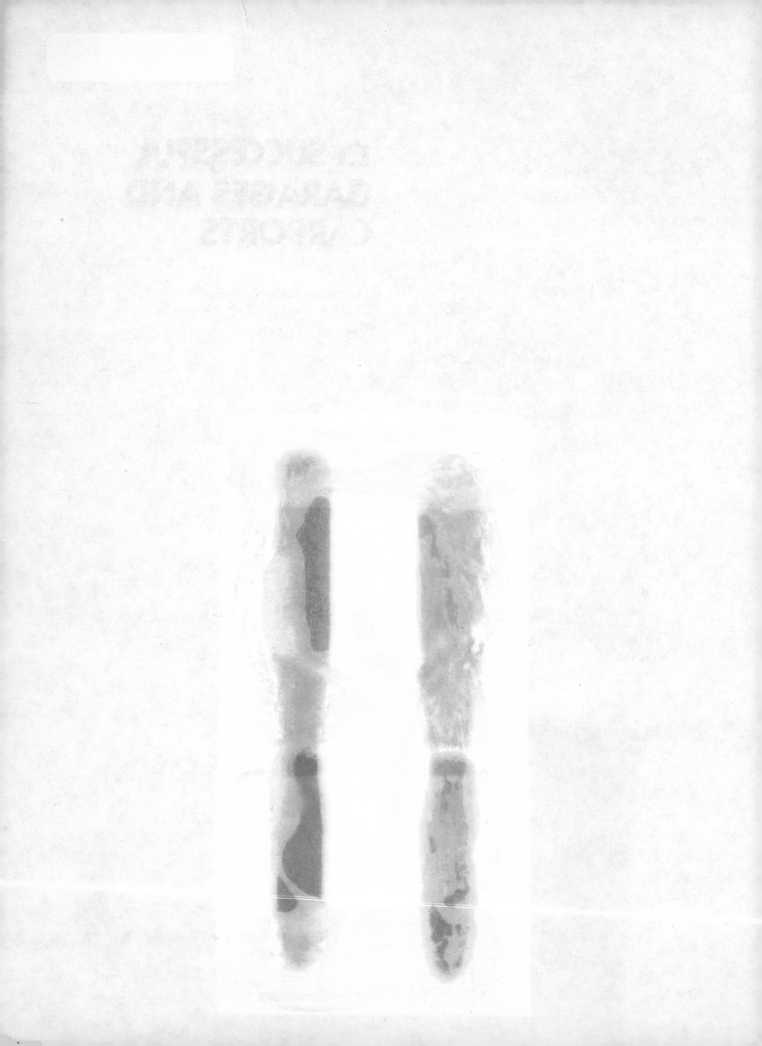

⌂ SUCCESSFUL GARAGES AND CARPORTS

Joseph F. Schram

Structures Publishing
Farmington, Michigan 48024

Manufactured in the United States of America

Edited by Virginia A. Case

Book design by Linda A. Zitzewitz

Cover photo courtesy of Home Planners, Inc.

Current Printing (last digit)
10 9 8 7 6 5 4 3 2 1

Structures Publishing Company
24277 Indoplex Circle
Box 1002, Farmington, Mich. 48024

ISBN 0-89999-018-5 {PAPER}

Library of Congress Cataloging in Publication Data

Schram, Joseph F.
  Successful garages & carports.

  Bibliography: p.
  Includes index.
  1. Garages — Design and construction — Amateurs' manuals. 2. Carports — Design and construction — Amateurs' manuals. I. Title.
TH4960.S32   690'.89   80-23515
  ISBN 0-89999-017-7
  ISBN 0-89999-018-5 (pbk.)

Contents

Proper scale and use of compatible materials are important factors in successful garage construction. This home's attached garage utilizes roofing, siding, brick and window styles and types used on the home itself. The blacktop driveway and garage apron slope to a drain for efficient water runoff. (Photo courtesy of U.S. Steel)

1
Planning the Garage or Carport

To many, a garage is simply a place to store an automobile when it is not in use. To others, a garage is a place that's a catch-all for out-of-use items with or without wheels — a collection most times barring any possibility of parking the car. For still other persons, a garage is a successful combination of storage areas for automobiles and seldom-used items, a convenient place to enjoy hobbies or undertake various household repairs, and a worthwhile enclosure kept in good order.

Those in need of garage space needn't wait. Building a garage is well within the ability of most persons handy with common carpenter tools and building materials. This type of project can easily be completed in several weeks during good building weather and is often an excellent summer vacation project that can involve the entire family.

Like any other home building improvement, it's mandatory that you answer a number of questions and determine a number of facts before you begin physical labor. Shortcutting this mental paperwork activity most often results in needless problems and a structure that doesn't provide as much as it should in these days of high construction costs.

Aside from cost, the paramount question to answer is whether or not your site is large enough and suitable (in the eyes of city government) for a garage. You must take into consideration all city setback restrictions and any other deed restrictions related to adding a new structure to your land. In some areas, for example, deed restrictions do not permit detached garages. Thus your existing space must be great enough to attach the new garage to the house and still be within rear, front and side setback lines.

Limitations of the site (its slope, location of the driveway, etc.) will help you to determine the best possible location as well as the basic type of garage — attached, detached, basement or carport. Where space is not a limitation, the attached garage has much in its favor. It may provide better architectural

lines to the house, it is warmer in the winter, and it provides covered protection to passengers, convenient space for storage, and a short, direct entrance to the house.

Building regulations often require that detached garages be located away from the house toward the rear of the lot. Where there is considerable slope to a lot, basement garages may be desirable. Generally such garages will cost less than those above grade if they are incorporated in the original house plans.

Another question of major importance is size. How many cars will your new garage accommodate? What other purposes do you intend for the garage?

It is a mistake to design the garage too small for convenient use. Cars vary in size from the small import models to larger and more expensive models almost 20 feet (6 meters) in length. Thus, while the garage need not be designed to take all sizes with adequate room around the car, it is wise to provide a minimum distance of 21 to 22 feet (6.4 to 6.7 meters) between the inside of the front and rear walls. If additional storage or work space is required at the back, a greater depth is required.

The inside width of a single garage should never be less than 11 feet (3.3 meters), with 13 feet (3.9 meters) or greater more satisfactory. The minimum outside size for a single garage, therefore, would be 14x22 feet (4.2x6.7 meters). A double garage should not be less than 22x22 feet (6.7x6.7 meters) in outside dimensions to provide reasonable clearance and use. The addition of a shop or storage area would increase these minimum sizes.

Your selection of garage design should be dictated by your house style. A new garage should be in total keeping with the house style, whether the vehicle structure is completed as part of the original house construction or as a later addition. Mixing a modern, flat-roof contemporary garage with a traditional colonial home can have an adverse affect on the re-sale value of the total property. Stick with your original style, always keeping in mind that the structure you are building is far too large to hide from view once it has been completed.

In speaking of house styles, a number of terms quickly come to mind: Colonial, Contemporary, Georgian, English Tudor, California ranch, Greek Revival, French Provincial, etc. But beyond these terms "style" also defines pattern, color and texture (PCT) and involves balance, scale and unity (BSU). More will be said in later chapters on the "PCT" group, but initial planning involving placement of the garage must take into consideration the "BSU" group at the outset.

Balance, in relation to a house, is achieved when design elements on one side equal those on the other side. There is balance when one side of the lot or house doesn't seem heavier than the other side. Scale and proportion can be defined as the relationship of an object or a space to another, or the relationship of a group of objects or spaces to another or to others. Unity is achieved when all of the "PCT" group, scale and proportion are combined in a way that they look as though they belong together as part of a single unit. Examples of such combinations are readily visible in the house-garage styles shown on pages 10-12 and 14-16. Examples of poor unity unfortunately can be found in most home communities, especially those in which the local planning and building departments permit "add-ons" that resemble loose parts from blocks and erector sets.

While most garage openings face the street (for all to view the contents), many home sites permit side-entrance or rear-entrance for a more pleasing street-side appearance. Such arrangements, of course, require a corner lot or added driveway and ample turn-around area.

Still another consideration in preliminary planning for a new garage is a determination of best possible energy conservation — both your's and nature's. Placing the garage to take the force of northwest winter winds will help to keep your home warm and lower fuel bills, while not blocking south-

Contemporary homes provide an opportunity to utilize the garage for purposes beyond automobile storage. This residence, designed by David R. Kingwill, AIA, for his own use, includes a sundeck atop the separate garage structure connected at a 45 degree angle with an overhead bridge walkway. Metal pipe railing was chosen for the bridge and interior stairs, contributing to the open feeling of the house. The siding is diagonally-applied Clear All Heart redwood. (Photo courtesy of California Redwood Association)

The Colonial styling of this home has been carried through in construction of the attached garage which utilizes the same siding pattern, windows, shutters, drainage system, roofing and panel-style garage door. A large circular vent has been installed in the gable for garage ventilation. (Photo courtesy of Stephenson Cupolas)

west summer breezes that help to cool your home. To save your energy, (especially in cold climates), the driveway should be as straight and short as possible and slope away from the garage and house. If this isn't possible, adequate drainage should be provided to carry off melting snow and water.

To initiate your garage building plans with a contractor or to do the work yourself, you will need a building permit. It is advisable at this point to prepare a scale drawing of your entire property locating both existing structures and your proposed garage addition.

AUTOMOBILE DIMENSIONS

The gasoline shortage and higher prices have caused many Americans to trade in their full-size automobiles for compacts and sub-compacts that are more fuel efficient. Doing so, of course, changes their space needs in terms of actual square footage required to store the car in a garage or carport. However, the Federal Housing Administration and others (including most city codes) require that a new garage or carport be constructed large enough to house a standard-size car even if the immediate use will be for a smaller car.

The Motor Vehicle Manufacturers Association publishes dimensions for passenger cars. These dimensions (and those available for foreign-made cars) indicate three size ranges of interest to most garage planners:

- **Standard cars** (Ford Mercury, Oldsmobile Cutlass, Pontiac Catalina) are 77.5 to 79.3 inches (1 968.5 to 2 014.2 mm) wide and 209 to 218 inches (5 308.6 to 5 537.2 mm) long. Overall height is 54.5 to 56.8 inches (1 384.3 to 1 442.7 mm).
- **Compact cars** (Plymouth Arrow, AMC Gremlin, Ford Pinto) are 60.4 to 63.4 inches (1 534.1 to 1 610.3 mm) wide, 162.6 to 169.9 inches (4 130 to 4 315.4 mm) long and 50.4 to 52.4 inches (1 280.1 to 1 330.9 mm) high.
- **Sub-Compact cars** (Volkswagen Rabbit, Datsun 210, Honda Civic) are 63.4 inches (1 610.3 mm) wide, 155.3 inches (3 944.6 mm) long and 55.5 inches (1 409.7 mm) high.

As you can see, there is very little difference in car height. Widths reduce by one to two feet (.3 to .6 meters) for smaller cars and the big difference is in length — 17+ feet (5.1+ meters) for standard, 13+ feet (3.9+ meters) for compact and 12+ feet (3.6+ meters) for sub-compacts.

Colonial

Cape Cod

Gambrel

French Mansard

French

English Tudor

**Choose a
Style
that suits
your home**

Cotswold

(Courtesy of Home Planners, Inc.)

Greek Revival *(Front)*

(Back)

Ranch

Spanish

Mansard Contemporary *(Front)*

(Back)

Geometric

(Courtesy of Home Planners, Inc.)

Georgian (Front) (Back)

Flat Roof Contemporary (Front) (Back)

Flat Roof Spanish

(Drawings courtesy of Home Planners, Inc.)

2
Garage Sizes and Types

A residential garage can vary in size from a one, two or three-car dimension or larger, depending upon owner need, property limitations, and, of course, cost. Many older homes were constructed with single-car units, while most newer homes are offered with two or three-car garages to handle a more mobile society.

Regardless of size, the new garage can easily be designed in one of more than a dozen specific styles, each of which has its own merits. Among these styles are:

- **Attached as an in-line.** This garage offers the advantage of a single roof line or may have a drop-down lower roof to lessen the visual length of the home.
- **Attached as an L-shape.** This style permits placement of the garage opening at either a right angle or directly opposite the street. An interior door from the garage usually gives immediate access to a utility room, mud room, lavatory or hallway which connects the garage to the service entrance of the home (pantry, kitchen area).
- **Attached as a front projection.** By being closer to the street, less driveway is required and the projection adds to the architectural appearance of the home by creating an L-shape planting or entrance area. Projected garages usually have one or more rooms beyond the back wall, with a door access through this wall to the laundry, family room, mud room, kitchen or hallway.
- **Attached as a rear projection.** Most frequently used with two-story home designs, this placement minimizes the garage structure in terms of street visibility, sometimes with the garage being completely behind the home and totally out of view. Here again, the interior garage door provides access to a service area or hallway

serving more active rooms in the home. Depending upon roof style, such designs can incorporate above-the-garage storage accessible by means of a disappearing stairway.

- **Attached as a balancing wing.** French, Colonial and Georgian-style homes often utilize this garage style to give desired balance to the total structure. When the garage opening doesn't directly face the street, windows are placed in the front wall to match size and placement of windows used in the opposite wing. Such side entry for the car requires a corner lot or more driveway area.
- **Attached as an angular shape.** Irregular-shaped lots, the desire for different and separate outdoor living areas, and greater curb appeal are several reasons for adopting this style. The garage almost always has an end entrance and can have either a roof line in continuation with the home or its own roof line.
- **Attached to help form a court.** Open garden or fully-enclosed entry courts can be established through such placement of the garage. A side passage door provides access from the garage to the court and this style home-garage usually requires multiple roof lines.
- **Attached under the house.** Hillside lots and multi-level home designs afford the opportunity to use a floor level above the garage for living area, either as bedrooms or family room, etc.
- **Attached on a corner lot.** Such homesites give the owner the opportunity to locate the garage at a right angle to the home and use different streets for auto and guest entry. Various rooms can be placed between garage and house, or this area can be used as a protected breezeway.
- **Attached with a breezeway.** Both straight-line and right-angle garage placement can include an attached breezeway. Careful placement of garage and home "people" doors will permit use of outdoor furniture in the breezeway.

13

Attached In-Line

Attached L-Shape

Attached Front Projection

Attached Rear Projection

Attached Balancing Wing

Attached Angular Shape

Attached Forming Court

Attached Under House

Courtesy of Home Planners, Inc.)

Attached on Corner Lot   (Front)

(Back)

Attached with Livability

Attached with Breezeway

Attached with Family Room

Attached Hobby Garage

Attached with Livability Under Same Roof   (Front)

(Back)

(Drawings courtesy of Home Planners, Inc.)

Garage as Part of Complex (Front)

(Back)

Attached New Addition to Period House (Front)

(Back)

(Courtesy of Home Planners, Inc.)

- **Attached with a family room.** Building a new garage can include an addition of a family room for the growing family. In such projects, access is provided from the garage to family room to kitchen or other adjoining rooms.
- **Attached as a hobby garage.** Including added space beyond that needed for car storage, this style garage can serve a wide range of hobby activities. Space can be along the sides, at the rear of the garage, or in all three places.
- **Attached with livability under the same roof.** Including separate rooms adjacent to the garage permits utilization of the same roof and lowers construction costs when comparing separate structures. Such added space could be used for storage area, laundry room or other purposes.
- **As part of complex.** Attached or unattached, the garage can take on a "separate" building appearance in a home design that dramatizes separate living areas.
- **Attached as an addition to a period house.** Careful attention must be given to architectural details so the new garage is accepted as part of the original structure. Siding, windows and roofing should match those used on the home.

PLANS AND SPECIFICATIONS

There are a variety of ways to obtain plans and specifications for building your garage. Hiring an architect or home designer is one option, but it can be quite expensive. A faster, simpler method is to browse through catalogs or plan books provided by stock plan services. These firms prepare books (from which you may order plans) containing simple floor plans and a sketch of the finished building. Please refer to *Ordering information for Plans* at the back of this book for the names of several stock plan suppliers.

In cooperation with the author, Home Planners, Inc., Farmington Hills, Michigan, has prepared complete plans and specifications for six highly functional garages which can be built by the homeowner or professional contractor. These garages range in size from a single-car to three-car size, each with different roof line and all with vital storage space.

The garage plans are available from the designers as a "ready-to-submit" package suitable for obtaining your building permit as well as ordering materials and, with the help of this book, accomplishing the construction.

One-Car Garag[e]

...Car Gable Roof

Traditional Two-Car

Two-Car Gable Roof, Front Opening

Two-Car with In-Line Roof, Side Opening   (Front)

(Back)

Two-Car Gable Roof, Side Opening

Contemporary Two-Car

(Courtesy of Home Planners, Inc.)

Three-Car, Side Opening   *(Front)*   *(Back)*

Three-Car, Front Opening   Three-Car, Partial Livability Above

(Drawings courtesy of Home Planners, Inc.)

Blueprints include:
- An artist's landscaped sketch of the exterior and ink-lined floor plan with basic exterior dimensions and square footage.
- Quarter-inch scale drawing of the foundation plan with all pertinent dimensions noted.
- Detailed elevations for all four sides of the garage with callouts for exterior materials including siding, doors, windows, roofing, flashing and gutters, and trim.
- Half-inch scale detail drawings pertaining to roof framing, cornice detail, door frames and wall assembly.
- A complete breakdown of material by type, size and quantity that will permit you to easily obtain cost estimates from local building materials dealers.

Here are a few highlights of the six plans illustrated on the following pages:

PLAN G-100: The largest plan in total square footage. This two-story structure has separate doors for two cars, heater room and storage or workshop area on the first level with a future apartment, study, playroom, etc., above. Gambrel roof design adds architectural interest and the second story can be equipped with kitchen and bath, local building codes permitting. Another option is a wood-burning fireplace and prefabricated chimney.

PLAN G-101: Totally conventional, this two-car garage has a single overhead door, matching side windows and a rear service door leading to the yard. Measuring 21 feet 5 inches x 23 feet 3 inches, (6.4 meters, 127 mm x 7 meters, 76.2 mm), the structure

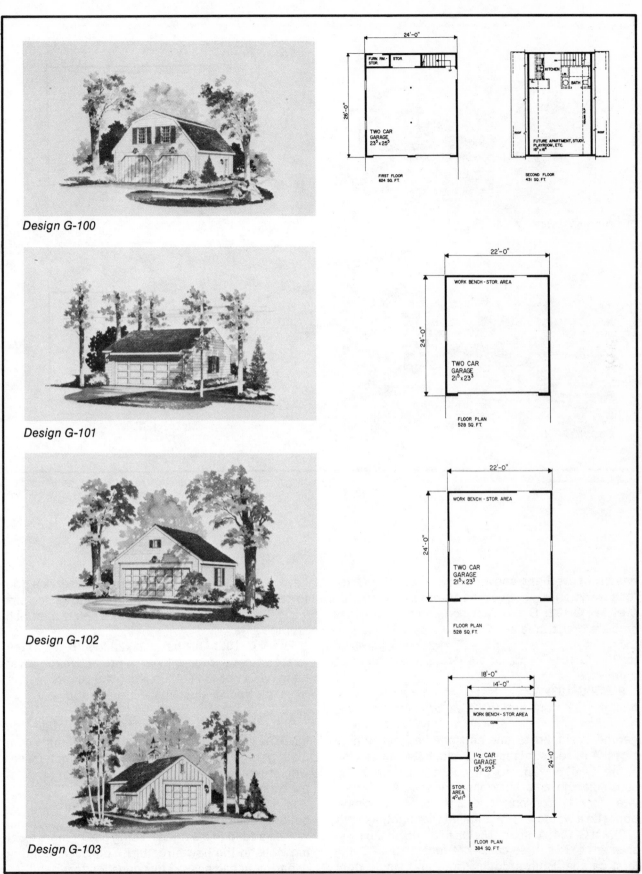

Design G-100

FURN. RM. - STOR.

STOR.

TWO CAR GARAGE
23⁵ x 25⁵

FIRST FLOOR
624 SQ. FT.

24'-0"

26'-0"

KITCHEN

BATH

FUTURE APARTMENT, STUDY, PLAYROOM, ETC.
16⁰ x 16⁵

ROOF

ROOF

SECOND FLOOR
431 SQ. FT.

Design G-101

WORK BENCH - STOR. AREA

TWO CAR GARAGE
21⁵ x 23³

22'-0"

24'-0"

FLOOR PLAN
528 SQ. FT.

Design G-102

WORK BENCH - STOR. AREA

TWO CAR GARAGE
21⁵ x 23³

22'-0"

24'-0"

FLOOR PLAN
528 SQ. FT.

Design G-103

WORK BENCH - STOR. AREA

CURB

1½ CAR GARAGE
13⁵ x 23⁵

STOR. AREA
4⁰ x 11³

18'-0"

14'-0"

24'-0"

FLOOR PLAN
384 SQ. FT.

(Courtesy of Home Planners, Inc.)

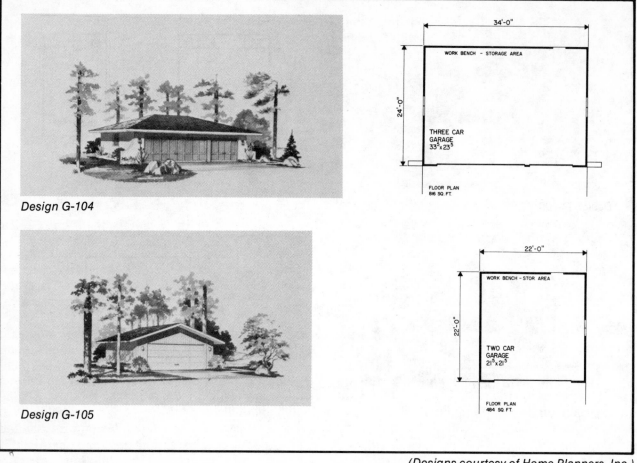

Design G-104

Design G-105

34'-0"

WORK BENCH - STORAGE AREA

24'-0"

THREE CAR
GARAGE
33⁵x23⁵

FLOOR PLAN
816 SQ. FT.

22'-0"

WORK BENCH - STOR. AREA

22'-0"

TWO CAR
GARAGE
21⁵x21⁵

FLOOR PLAN
484 SQ. FT.

(Designs courtesy of Home Planners, Inc.)

has a roof overhang above the main door and space for a workbench-storage area across the rear wall.

PLAN G-102: Gable roof construction provides ample storage area above the two-car, 528-square foot (49 square meters) plan. The interior is identical to Plan G-101, with roof construction as the main difference.

PLAN G-103: A 4x11 feet 5 inch (1.2 meters x 3.3 meters, 127 mm) storage area projects from the front side of this basic 14x24 foot (4.2x7.3 meters) garage designed to one and one-half car dimensions. A raised concrete curb is detailed across the entire garage width to provide a separate workbench-storage area along the rear wall. A side service door is convenient to the yard and almost opposite a window for natural interior lighting.

PLAN G-104: A hip roof helps to diminish the massiveness of this three-car 34x24-foot (10.3 x 7.3 meters) garage. Both a double-door and single door

have been specified for the entrance, a service door for the rear wall and matching windows for side walls. The long rear wall provides a fine workbench-storage area.

PLAN G-105: This basic 22x22 foot (6.7x6.7 meters) two-car garage with large protective roof overhang has a net 484 square feet (44.9 square meters) of usable space, plus limited storage above.

Still other garage plans are available, often from local building materials dealers who assemble complete garage packages for sale to the homeowner, who must then obtain concrete and labor for complete assembly.

In some areas, the services of an architect or building designer may be required if the new garage is to be added to the house, using one or more existing walls in the new structure. Your local building department can answer this question for you.

3
Driveways

The proper planning and construction of your driveway may already have been done for you at the time your home was built. But in most instances involving the construction of a new garage or carport, driveway changes and improvements will be required.

Local regulations generally specify what you can and cannot do with the "apron area" and "parking strip" (the narrow piece of land between curb and sidewalk), but the balance of the driveway design remains in your control.

Driveways for single-car garages or carports are usually 10 to 14 feet (3 to 4.2 meters) wide, with a minimum 14-foot (4.2 meters) width for curving drives. In all instances, the driveway should be three feet (.9 meters) wider than the widest vehicle it will serve.

Long driveway approaches to multiple-car garages may be single-car width, but must be widened near the garage to provide access to each stall. Short driveways for two-car garages should be 16 to 24 feet (4.8 to 7.3 meters) wide and 28 to 30 feet (8.5 to 9.1 meters) for three-car garages.

Safety is a key factor in all driveway design and it is recommended that driveways not be located immediately at the corner of the house, behind trees or high shrubs. Care should be taken that the car operator has full visibility of sidewalk pedestrians and street vehicles when backing the car from the drive into the street.

In some instances it will be well worth the yard space involved to provide a turn-around or turning "Y" or "T" to totally eliminate the need to back a car from driveway to street. The basic "Y" for turning purposes for a straight driveway requires a minimum of 15 feet (4.5 meters) and a maximum of 20 feet (6 meters) between the edge of the garage and the property line, landscaping or other obstruction.

In studies conducted by the University of Illinois Small Homes Council, it has been determined that driveways leading to side-entrance garages require an extension approximately eight feet (2.4 meters)

Decorative planting can be a featured part of the driveway when lot size permits a circular layout. This driveway is further beautified through the use of exposed aggregate concrete. (Photo courtesy of Portland Cement Association)

The beauty and efficiency of this ample-size concrete driveway is partially marred by the use of bushy landscaping at the curb edge. This provides a visibility hazard in backing out of the drive. Plantings at this position should be low and unobstructive. (Photo courtesy of Portland Cement Association)

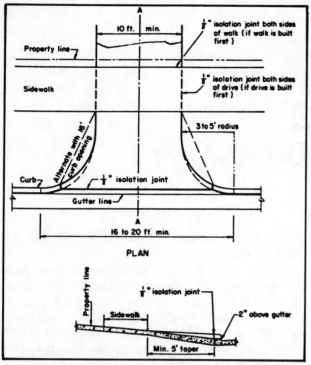

The driveway entrance varies from home to home depending upon presence or absence of public sidewalk and type of curb. This typical plan, recommended by the Portland Cement Association, calls for a minimum 10-foot-wide (3 meters) driveway with a minimum 16 to 20-foot (4.8 to 6 meters) curb opening.

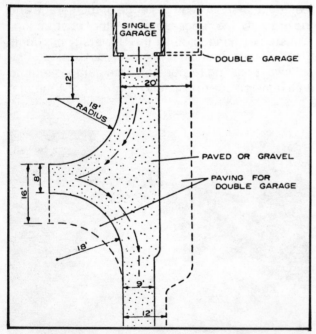

Use of a driveway turning "T" avoids many hazards. A minimum of 15 feet (4.5 meters) and a maximum of 20 feet (6 meters) is required between the edge of the garage and the property line. The bottom dimension of the "T" should be no less than eight feet (2.4 meters), preferably 10 feet (3 meters) for a single-car garage and 16 feet (4.8 meters) for a double garage. (Drawing courtesy of Portland Cement Association)

beyond the farthest edge of the garage and widening to a minimum 23 feet (7 meters) in front of the entrance to permit easy in/out car movement.

The minimum outside radius for a single curved drive depends upon the width of the drive:

Width	Minimum Outside Radius
9'6'' (2.7 meters, 152.4 mm)	55' (16.7 meters)
10'6'' (3 meters, 152.4 mm)	31' (9.4 meters)
11'6'' (3.3 meters, 152.4 mm)	24'9''(7.3 meters, 228.6 mm)

Rear-entrance garages require less side yard and less driveway width than side-entrance garages, but do require more backyard space — approximately 36 to 40 feet (10.9 to 12.1 meters) toward the rear lot line and 35 feet to 38 feet 6 inches (10.6 meters to 11.5 meters, 152.4 mm) from the right-hand garage wall toward the outside lot line.

Semi-circular driveways work better with front-entrance garages than with side-entrance ones. These driveways afford one-way-in and one-way-out, but require lots large enough to utilize a 10-foot-wide (3 meters) drive with an 18-foot (5.4 meters) turning radius. A complete circle turnaround requires a minimum inside radius of 19 to 20 feet (5.7 to 6 meters).

If the garage is considerably above or below street level and is located near the street, the driveway grade may be critical. A grade of 14 percent (1-3/4-inch or 44 mm vertical rise for each running foot or 300 mm) is the maximum that is recommended. The change in grade should be gradual to avoid scraping the car's bumper or underside. The most critical point occurs when the rear wheels are in the gutter as the vehicle approaches a driveway from the street.

Driveways that are of necessity quite steep should have a near-level area in front of the garage for safety, from 12 to 16 feet (3.6 to 4.8 meters) long. Driveways that have a grade of more than seven percent (7 feet or 2.1 meters rise in 100 feet or 30.4 meters) should have some type of pavement to prevent wash.

A slope of 1/4-inch (6 mm) per running foot (300 mm) is recommended by the Portland Cement Association, with the direction of the slope depending upon local conditions, usually toward the street. A crown or cross-slope may be used for drainage where garage-to-street drainage is impossible.

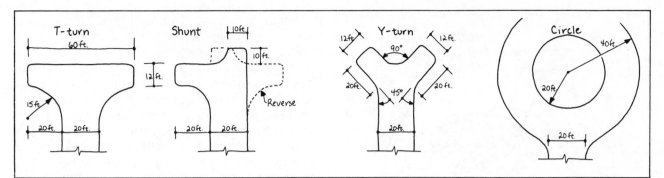

Driveway "Y" and circular turns make forward-in and forward-out auto movement to and from the garage possible. Likewise, semi-circular drive-arounds can be used if space permits a 30 to 32-foot (9.1 to 9.7 meters) outside diameter and 19 to 21-foot (5.7 to 6.4 meters) inside diameter. (Drawings courtesy of HUD's Manual of Acceptable Practices)

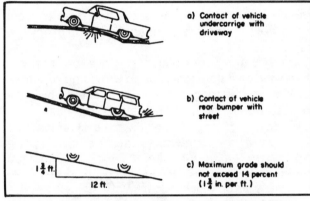

Garages above or below street level require special attention to the grade. This way the change in grade is gradual and does not cause the car's bumper or underside to scrape. A grade of 14 percent (1.3/4-inch or 44 mm vertical rise for each running foot or 300 mm) is the maximum recommended by the Portland Cement Association. The most critical point is when the rear wheels are in the gutter as vehicles approach the driveway from the street.

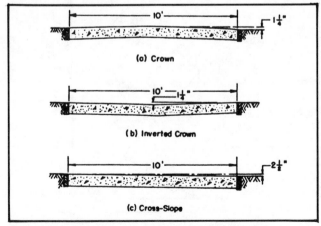

Efficient drainage is accomplished by building the driveway with a slope of 1/4-inch (6 mm) per running foot (300 mm) toward the street. However, side drainage can be accomplished using any of these three methods: crown, inverted crown, or cross-slope. (Drawing courtesy of Portland Cement Association)

Concrete and bituminous (blacktop) pavement are most commonly used in areas where snow removal is important. In some areas of the country, a gravel driveway and a flagstone walk may be satisfactory and a means of reducing construction costs.

Two types of paved driveways may be used: the more common slab or full-width type, and the ribbon type with a grass strip between runners. When driveways are fairly long or steep, the full-width type is more practical. The ribbon driveway is cheaper but impractical for curved drives and poses more problems in snow country. The concrete strips in a ribbon driveway should be at least two feet (.6 meters) wide and located so they are five feet (1.5 meters) on center (from the center of one strip to the center of the other). When the ribbon also is used as a walk, the width of the strips should be increased to at least

Basic principles of driveway construction are shown here – good width, turn-around space and ample entrance swing from the street. (Photo courtesy of Portland Cement Association)

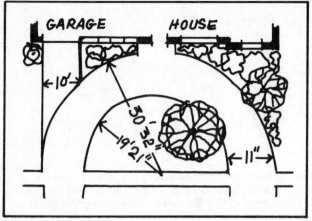

A semi-circular driveway is most desirable when it eliminates the need to back into busy street traffic. This arrangement permits the owner to enter the garage using the left approach, back out of the garage to the turn-around and exit the property in a forward direction, via the drive at the right. (Courtesy of Frantz Manufacturing)

three feet (.9 meters). For full-width driveways used as walks, add another two feet (.6 meters) to the minimum 10-foot (3 meters) width.

The part of the driveway between street and public sidewalk is usually controlled by the local municipality. Officials should be consulted after the street, curbs and public walks are in place. If the curb and gutter have not been installed, it is advisable to end the driveway temporarily at the public sidewalk or property line. An entry of gravel or crushed stone can be used until curbs and gutter are built. At that time, the drive entrance can be completed with the apron having a three to five-foot (.9 to 1.5 meters) radius to the driveway sidelines.

If the driveway is built before the public walk, it should meet the sidewalk grade and drop to meet the gutter (if no curb is planned) or the top of any low curb.

In completing your plans for a new or improved driveway, give consideration to providing off-street parking spaces for guests and youngsters who grow into teens and begin adding cars to your fleet.

When angled on a 22-foot (6.7 meters) radius from the edge of your driveway surface, additional parking spaces require a minimum 24-foot (7.3 meters)

Precast concrete slabs also can be used for driveway construction with careful attention given to the subbase and proper slope for drainage. (Photo courtesy of Portland Cement Association)

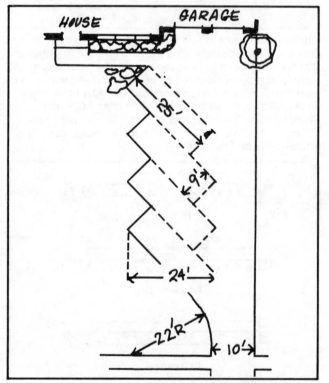

Guest parking stalls can be provided best with a 22-foot (6.7 meters) radius off the home's driveway. Spaces should be a minimum 9-feet wide (2.7 meters), with 20 feet (6 meters) to wheel line and 25 feet (7.6 meters) to bumper line. Such parking should not interfere with the 10-foot (3 meters) width of the driveway itself. (Courtesy of Frantz Manufacturing)

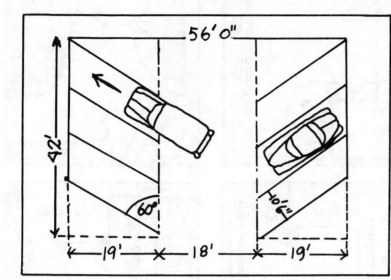

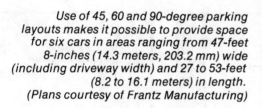

Use of 45, 60 and 90-degree parking layouts makes it possible to provide space for six cars in areas ranging from 47-feet 8-inches (14.3 meters, 203.2 mm) wide (including driveway width) and 27 to 53-feet (8.2 to 16.1 meters) in length. (Plans courtesy of Frantz Manufacturing)

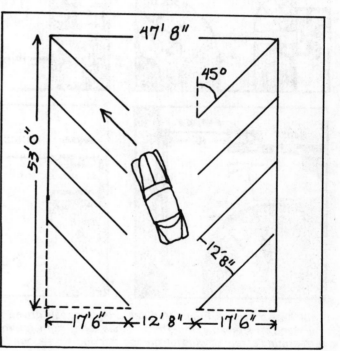

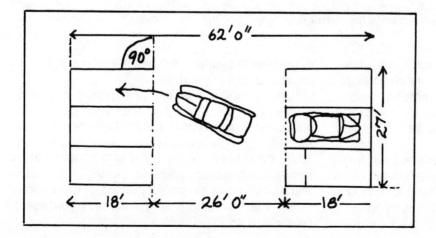

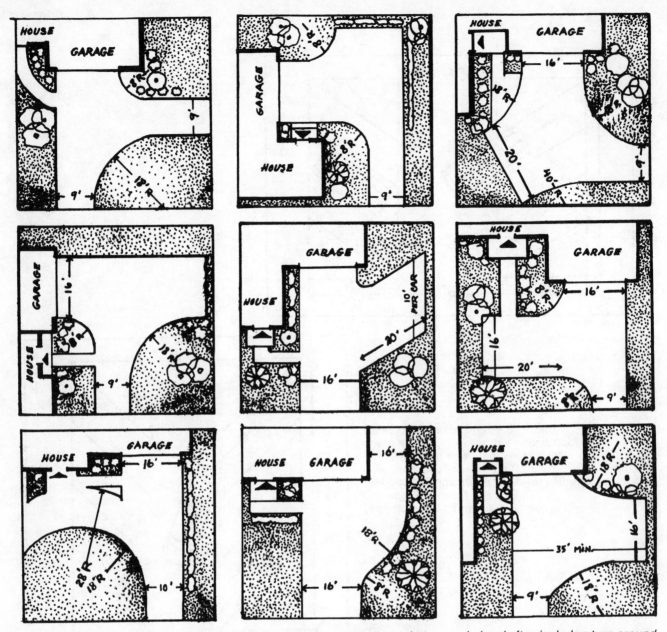

In these drawings, Frantz Manufacturing suggests driveway patterns that are varied and often include a turn-around and off-street parking. The sketches, left to right, top row include: entrance, exit for a corner lot; garage, parking, turn-around at rear of wide lot; garage, parking, turn-around at front for corner lot; middle row, garage at rear with side turn-around and parking for wide lot; garage, parking, turn-around at front for average lot; garage, parking, turn-around at front for narrow lot; bottom row, garage at front with circular drive for narrow corner lot; parking, turn-around beside garage for narrow lot; garage, parking, turn-around at front for average lot.

wide strip. A "stop" can be set in each space at approximately 20 feet (6 meters) from the drive edge, allowing the front bumper area to extend another five feet (1.5 meters) toward plants or grass. The width of each parking space should be a minimum nine feet (2.7 meters).

Still another consideration in planning your driveway and guest parking is landscaping. Keep in mind that low-hanging trees and protruding shrubs can scrape and damage car surfaces. Overhanging trees also may have sap or fruit droppings at various times

of the year in addition to being great "rest stops" for your local bird population.

Keep in mind that ample time spent in planning a driveway will be well rewarded. Once concrete or blacktop has been poured and sets, it becomes most difficult and expensive to start making changes that could have been made so easily on paper beforehand. Using wood stakes to outline your "paper plans" on the site will permit you to test it completely to see that everything is just the way you want it before construction begins.

4
Layout

Following acceptance of your garage plan and receipt of a building permit from the local municipality, you are ready to begin construction. It's recommended, if possible, this construction be undertaken in the best building season to avoid the extremely hot days (which cause concrete problems), extended rainy periods and, of course, snow.

The first step in building is to stake out the corner and wall lines and erect batter boards. You may wish to rent a surveyor's transit or employ the services of a professional surveyor who will do the staking for you.

The accompanying sketches by Johns-Manville illustrate a typical layout plan for a two-car garage measuring 21-feet 2-inches (6.4 meters, 50.8 mm) wide and 22-feet 6-inches (6.7 meters, 152.4 mm) long. This layout technique can be adjusted to other dimensions.

When you do it yourself, first establish the back line of the garage (Figure 1, line A-B) which in this design is 21-feet 2-inches (6.4 meters, 50.8 mm)

long. Drive in stakes at the corners of the line so that the corner points will be at the approximate centers of the stakes. Drive nails into the corner stakes at the exact corner points.

Along line A-B, six feet (1.8 meters) from stake "A," drive stake "E." Then drive a nail in stake "E" exactly six feet (1.8 meters) from the nail in stake "A." Next drive stake "F" at a point eight feet (2.4 meters) from stake "A" and 10 feet (3 meters) from stake "E," driving a nail in stake "F" at the exact corner point.

Doing this will give you an exact "A-E-F" right triangle. Now extend line "A-F" to "D." Drive a stake at "D" and a nail in the stake exactly 22-feet 6-inches (6.7 meters, 152.4 mm) from the nail in stake "A." Establish the other two corners of the garage in the same way. To check your procedure, measure diagonals "A-C" and "B-D." They should be equal.

It is now time to erect the batter boards as illustrated in Figure 1, leveling all top lines of the boards with a line level. It is most important that the top lines of all batter boards be at the same level. Batter

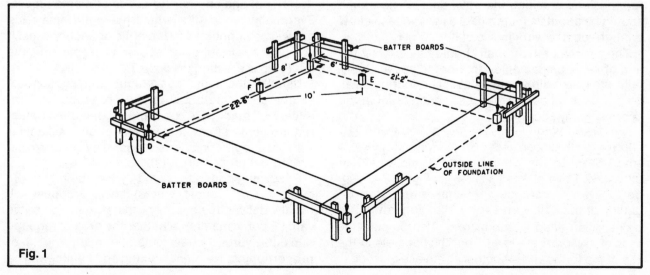

Fig. 1

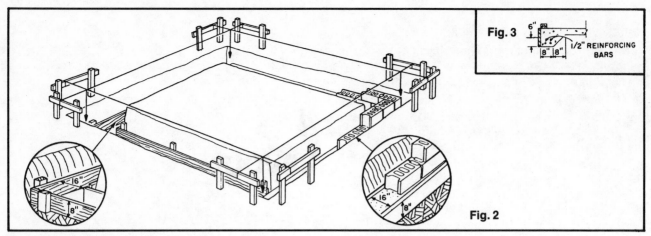

Fig. 3

1/2" REINFORCING BARS

Fig. 2

(Drawings courtesy of Johns-Manville)

boards should be far enough away from the outside line of the foundation in order to do the excavation work.

Stretch mason's strings across the batter boards as shown to intersect exactly over the nails in stakes "A," "B," "C" and "D." Nails should be driven into the batter boards where the strings are fastened, so new strings can be fastened in case the original ones are broken.

As shown in Figure 1, suspend plumb bobs (pointed weights) as corner points over nails in stakes. This should be where the string intersects at the corners. Then remove stakes "A," "B," "C," "D," "E" and "F" so that you can excavate a trench for the footing. Since the footing must project four inches (101.6 mm) beyond the wall line, stretch a second line across the batter boards four inches (101.6 mm) outside the lines previously established for the walls. Drop plumb lines from these new outside corners to establish the corners for the footings.

It is now time to excavate a trench around the perimeter of the garage to a depth at least eight inches (203.2 mm) below the frost line in your area. This is most important to prevent frost from heaving footings and cracking the walls above. The trench should be about 24 inches (609.6 mm) wide to allow enough room to work inside of it.

The bottom of the trench should be perfectly flat and of well compacted earth. Should you accidentally excavate below your established footing level, do not back fill such areas. Let concrete fill in the depth actually excavated.

Next, build wood forms for the footing using 1x8 (19x184 mm) lumber as shown in Figure 2. Leave a space between the lumber forms 16 inches (406.4 mm) wide. Drive stakes as shown in Figure 2 to support the form. Make sure the stakes are close together or back fill with earth so the forms will not bulge when filled with concrete. Also be sure the tops of the forms are level. Pour the concrete to the top of the forms and smooth with a piece of wood.

Wood forms for footings are not necessary in stable soils such as clay or shale, because the earth trench itself will hold together and serve as a form. In such cases excavate carefully to allow for a footing 16 inches (406.4 mm) wide and extending eight inches (203.2 mm) below the frost line.

[If you live in an area where the frost penetration is not a problem, excavate a trench six inches (152.4 mm) deep for the footing (Figure 3). Build a form of 1x12 (19x286 mm) lumber for just the outside of the footing so that the inside face of the form is on a line with the established outside dimensions of the garage. Then pour the footing and the garage floor at the same time.

As shown in Figure 3, install two 1/2-inch (12.7 mm) round steel reinforcing bars around the perimeter of the footing before pouring the concrete. Also place 1/2x15-inch (12.7x381 mm) threaded foundation bolts in the footing to a depth of 10 inches (254 mm), and spaced eight feet (2.4 meters) apart (or follow local building code), while pouring the concrete. Anchor clips can be used as an alternate to bolts. The Panel Clip Company offers anchor clips in two sizes — one kind for use in concrete (as just described) and another for use in concrete blocks. Eventually, wood sills (which the wall frame rests on) will be connected to the bolts or anchor clips. If you pour the footing and floor at the same time, the next step is erecting the walls.]

Usually, the most convenient and economical source of concrete is a ready mix producer. Producers of ready mix can supply concrete to meet requirements of any project and often are familiar with local soil conditions. Thus, they can provide exactly the proper mix for the use involved.

Ready mix concrete is sold by the cubic yard (27 cubic feet or .7 cubic meters), and a producer will usually deliver any quantity greater than one cubic yard (.7 cubic meters). Whether the project requires one cubic yard (.7 cubic meters) or many, the job of proportioning, weighing, mixing and hauling will be done according to careful specifications to insure concrete of uniform quality.

The cost of ready mixed concrete varies with distance hauled, size of order, day of delivery, unloading time, and type of mix. A call to one or more reputable producers should be made to establish the local price.

In some cases, if the quantity of concrete needed is less than one cubic yard (.7 cubic meters) or if there is no ready mix plant in the area, it will be necessary to make the concrete on the job. For footings, you can use one bag of cement to 5-1/2 gallons (20.8 L) of water. Add about 2-3/4 cubic feet (.07 cubic meters) of sand and four cubic feet (.11 cubic meters) of gravel (graded from 1-1/2 inches (38.1 mm) in size down). Note the proportion of sand and gravel can be varied to make a workable mushy type cement. The amount of water per bag should not be changed.

After the footing has set (about 24 hours), remove the forms and sweep the top clean before laying the concrete blocks if this type foundation wall is selected. (You may wish to make the entire foundation wall concrete to the point of the mud sill.) The concrete foundation wall should be composed of 8x8x16-inch (200x200x400 mm) blocks centered on the footing and lined up with the predetermined outside wall lines. Corners are determined by the strings on your batter boards.

Most garage builders prefer to use three-core stretcher blocks for the foundation wall, except at the corners and for the top course (top layer). At the corners, 8x8x16-inch (200x200x400 mm) corner blocks are used and the top course is solid top

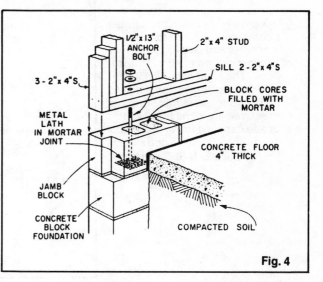

Fig. 4

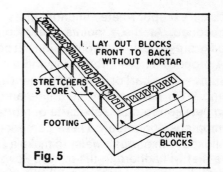

Fig. 5

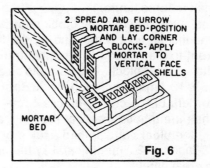

Fig. 6

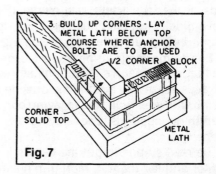

Fig. 7

(Drawings courtesy of Johns-Manville)

Using anchor clips is one way of securing wood to masonry. Two sizes are available – 14-3/4-inches (374.6 mm) for concrete or one block embedment, and 22-3/4-inches (577.8 mm) for going through two layers of concrete block. (Drawings courtesy of The Panel Clip Co.)

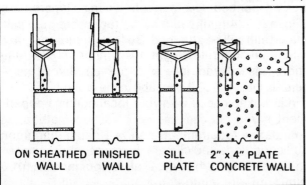

ON SHEATHED WALL   FINISHED WALL   SILL PLATE   2" x 4" PLATE CONCRETE WALL

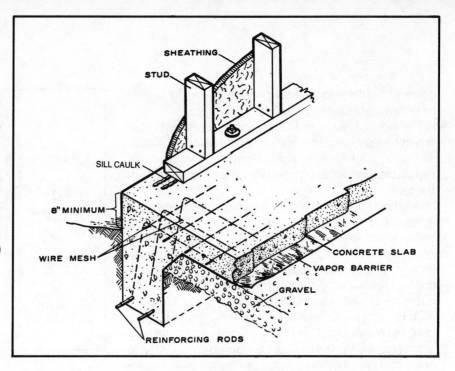

This cut-away drawing illustrates a combined slab and foundation of concrete and details placement of reinforcing rods and wire mesh. The eight inch (203.2 mm) minimum is from rough grade to top of concrete surface to allow the required six inches (152.4 mm) of space between finish grade and wood siding.
(Courtesy U.S. Department of Agriculture)

blocks except where anchor bolts are to be embedded. At these points, three-core stretcher blocks are used and later filled in with concrete.

A proper mix of mortar for laying the block is by volume — one part of Portland cement and between 1 and 1-1/4 parts of hydrated lime and lime putty, and between four and six parts of mortar sand in a damp, loose condition. These components should be mixed with enough water to make a sticky mix — one that will adhere to the trowel. Power mixing of mortar is preferred to hand mixing, but only enough mortar should be mixed to be used in the following two and one-half to three hours.

Following the layout of concrete block shown in Figure 5, start at the left front corner and lay the first blocks from front to rear without mortar, beginning and ending with a corner block. There should be 3/8 to 1/2-inch (9.5 to 12.7 mm) from each block. Be sure the outside corners of the corner blocks come directly under the plumb bobs. Then, at the left front corner, pick up the blocks and spread a full mortar bed (about 1/2-inch or 12.7 mm thick). Lay the corner block with great care.

Stand the other blocks on end and spread the ends of the face shells with mortar (Figure 6). Lay these blocks in place pushing them down into the mortar bed so as to leave a 3/8 to 1/2-inch (9.5 to 12.7 mm) mortar joint between the previously laid block. Use a mason's level to make certain the top surfaces are level and that the outside surfaces are plumb with your wall line. In laying concrete blocks, everything depends upon laying the first course properly.

The next step is to put the blocks in the left rear corner and lay them in mortar in a similar fashion. Then build up the left front and the left rear corners

(Figure 7) to the required height, depending on the depth of the foundation which has been predetermined by the frost conditions in your locality.

The top surface of the top course should be about eight inches (203.2 mm) above grade. Having built the corners level and plumb, lay the rest of the wall between the corners.

Next build up the right rear corner and fill in the rear wall of the garage. Then proceed to build up the right front corner and lay in the right wall.

The short front walls are best laid last with jamb blocks at the ends of the top course (Figure 4). These are used to allow an upward acting door to fall to the garage floor.

Some garage builders prefer to pour the foundation and concrete slab as an integral unit, as this construction method reduces the required amount of form work and further simplifies actual concrete placement.

Referred to as "rat wall" construction in some parts of the country, this one-pour operation usually calls for footings to be poured to a 12-inch (304.8 mm) depth (or below the frost line) with a base width of 12 inches (304.8 mm) and reinforcing as previously described. The foundation can be tapered to a 6-inch (152.4 mm) width at the top where mud sills (wood sill) will be attached. Building codes require a minimum concrete height of six inches (152.4 mm) above finished grade level so as to keep all wood members six inches (152.4 mm) above the ground.

It is well to check with your local building department if you choose this construction method, as foundation requirements can vary depending upon soil conditions and climate. Likewise, codes vary as to slab thickness, but most call for four inches (101.6 mm) with wire reinforcement.

5
Garage Floors

Like the driveway, the best time to construct a concrete slab garage or carport floor is early in the construction season before the hot days of summer. Any required sewer or water lines should be in place and connected, and the concrete slab should not be poured on recently filled areas.

Usual practice is to make the garage floor four inches (101.6 mm) thick and slope it from rear to front 1/8-inch (3 mm) per foot (300 mm) to allow easy wash down and drainage. Most building codes do not permit use of a floor drain as gasoline or gasoline fumes could accumulate and cause a fire hazard. If one is permitted, never connect it to the sewer system or septic tank — always join it to a dry well.

Before erecting form work for pouring the new concrete floor, remove all vegetation, loose earth, mud and organic materials from the sub-grade. Remove all soggy or soft spots and replace with dry earth, cinders, slag or gravel. A well-compacted foundation of four to six inches (101.6 to 152.4 mm) in depth will usually suffice.

If the foundation wall was constructed as previously detailed, use a chalk line to mark the height of the finished floor which is to be four inches (101.6 mm) above the sub-grade. Make certain that all lines are the same level and that you have created the pitch of 1/8-inch (3 mm) per foot (300 mm) toward the garage entrance. This means the floor will be higher in the back than in the front.

Next, place a 1/2-inch (12.7 mm) expansion joint (made from a folded thickness of roofing felt) along the sides and back of the foundation wall with the top of the felt lined up with the chalk lines you have made. Then place 2x4 (38x89 mm) lumber forms against the felt, staking them firmly in place. Place another 2x4 (38x89 mm) form down the middle of the garage and another across the door entry area. All these forms should be the same level as the chalk marks on the sides of the garage.

To estimate the amount of concrete you will need, in cubic yards, you multiply the area (in square feet) by the slab thickness (in fraction of a foot) and divide by 27.

For example, a 4-inch slab that is 10 feet wide and 12 feet long gives 120 square feet or surface, times 1/3 of a foot thickness, divided by 27. The net is 1.48

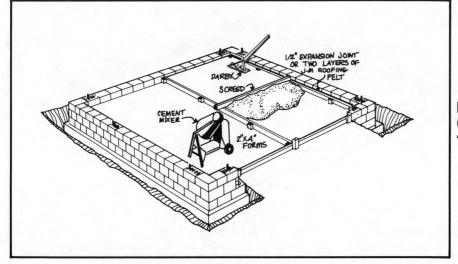

LAYING THE FOUNDATION
(Drawing courtesy of Johns-Manville)

cubic yards (1.1 cubic meters). But to allow for variations in subgrade and waste, it would be better to place the order for two cubic yards (1.5 cubic meters). This formula cannot be used when substituting metric numbers.

Ready-mix suppliers can provide you with the proper mix best suited to your locale and the construction purpose. Generally, this mixture for a garage floor will be five or six sacks of cement per cubic yard, aggregate no larger than one inch (25.4 mm) and six percent entrained air. Not more than six gallons (22.7 L) of mixing water should be used per bag of cement.

Many contractors and homeowners choose to reinforce the concrete slab with welded wire fabric to minimize cracking and crack sizes. A suitable fabric for this purpose is 6x6 (# 8/8) which is available from building material dealers in five or six-foot (1.5 or 1.8 meters) wide rolls or sheets. The material is positioned slightly above the center of the slab thickness on wire bar supports which hold the reinforcing in place when the concrete is poured.

If you plan to mix your own concrete, a suggested mix for the garage floor is, by volume, one part Portland Cement to 2-1/4 parts of sand and three parts of gravel or crushed stone. To this mix add six gallons (22.7 L) of water per bag of cement.

If you purchase ready-mix, be certain all your form work is securely in place and you are ready for the shipment when it arrives. The subgrade should be thoroughly dampened with water in advance to prevent absorption of water from the concrete. Rapid extraction of water from the concrete will seriously impair its strength.

Ready-mix trucks weigh from 18 to 22 tons (16 to 20 metric tons) and could cause damage to an existing driveway, sidewalk or lawn. Use of 2x12-inch (38x286 mm) planks for the truck to drive on can help to prevent ruts. If the truck cannot get to the pouring location, wheelbarrows will be required, or perhaps the ready-mix supplier can provide a pumping system to place the concrete by hose.

Depending upon your available manpower, you may choose to pour the entire floor at one time or half of it (as indicated in Figure 9) and the remainder when the first half has set.

As the concrete is poured, a 2x4 (38x89 mm) wood screed or strikeboard is pulled across the surface with a saw-like motion to level the concrete, using the tops of the forms as a guide. After screeding, the concrete should be smoothed with a long-handle wood float or darby.

The 2x4 (38x89 mm) forming used along the side and back walls is removed after three or four hours, before the concrete sets. The void between the cement and the felt is filled with concrete which is smoothed with a darby. The center, rear-to-front and across-the-front 2x4 (38x89 mm) forms remain in place, with only the center 2x4 (38x89 mm) removed before the start of the second concrete pour. This 2x4 (38x89 mm) is replaced with a 1/2-inch (12.7 mm) expansion joint made of folded roofing felt. The roofing felt also is used against the back and side walls in the same manner as the first pour.

Strikeoff is the operation of removing concrete not required to fill the forms and bringing the surface to grade. The tool used is known as a straightedge or strikeoff. Straightedges are made of wood

(Drawing courtesy of Johns-Manville)

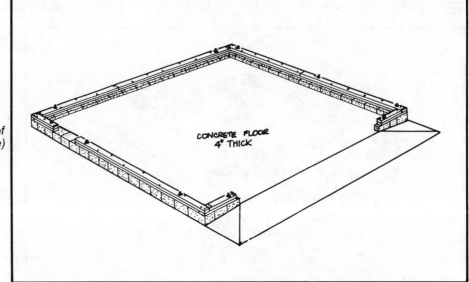

CONCRETE FLOOR 4" THICK

The poured concrete garage floor slab is struck off by moving a length of 2x4 (38x89 mm) lumber back and forth with a saw-like motion. The straightedge rests on the top edge of the formwork at each side of the section being finished. (Photo courtesy of Portland Cement Association)

Two types of darbies used to float the surface of a concrete slab are pictured here. This operation takes place immediately after the slab has been screeded. (Photos courtesy of Goldblatt Tool Co., and Portland Cement Association)

or metal. For small jobs like a garage floor, straight 2x4 (38x89 mm) lumber is an adequate replacement.

When using the straightedge, a small amount of concrete should be kept ahead of it to fill in low spots. About 30 inches (762 mm) should be covered in the first pass. As the straightedge is pulled forward, it should be tilted to obtain a cutting edge. If needed, a second pass should be made to remove any remaining bumps or low spots. During the second pass the straightedge should be tilted in the opposite direction.

Darbying immediately follows the strikeoff. The purpose of this operation is to level the ridges and fill voids left by the straightedge and to embed all particles of coarse aggregate slightly below the surface. A bull float is used for areas too large to reach with a darby; otherwise a darby is used.

Bull floats are large, long-handled tools made of wood or metal. The bull float should be pushed ahead with the front (toe) of the float raised so that it will not dig into the concrete surface. The tool should be pulled back with the float blade on the surface to cut off the bumps and fill holes. If holes or depressions remain and no excess concrete is left on the slab, additional concrete should be shoveled from a wheelbarrow and the surface bull-floated again.

Use of an edger produces a neat, rounded edge and prevents chipping or damage, especially when concrete forms are removed. Edging also compacts and hardens the concrete surface next to the form where floats and trowels are less effective. (Photos courtesy of Portland Cement Association)

This sidewalk construction view shows how a control joint can be cut with a groover, using a straight board as a guide. The groover should extend into the slab one-fourth to one-fifth of the slab thickness. It is good practice to mark the location of each joint with a string or chalk line on both sides of the forms and on the concrete surface. (Photo courtesy of Portland Cement Association)

Coarse-textured brooms can be used on newly floated concrete to give an interesting and functional texture. Medium to fine textures are achieved with soft-bristle brooms. (Photo courtesy of Portland Cement Association)

Darbies are hand-operated wood or metal tools, three to eight feet (.9 to 2.4 meters) long, three to four inches (76.2 to 101.6 mm) wide, with a handle on top. The long, flat, rectangular tool is held flat against the surface of the concrete and worked front right to left, or vice versa, with a sawing motion, cutting off bumps and filling depressions. When the surface is level, the darby should be tilted slightly and moved from right to left, or vice versa, to fill any holes made by the sawing motion.

These procedures should level and smooth the surface, working up a slight amount of concrete paste. Do not overwork the concrete as this will result in a less durable surface.

The Portland Cement Association cautions all who work with concrete not to spread the material over too large an area before strikeoff. Nor should a large area be struck off and allowed to remain before darbying. Any operation peformed on the surface of a concrete slab while water is present will cause the hardened concrete to flake or scale. This point cannot be overemphasized. It is the basic rule for successful finishing of concrete flatwork.

While a smooth-troweled concrete slab may be easy to clean, it's often slippery when wet. For this reason a garage floor should be broomed to produce a non-slip surface.

Broomed finishes are attractive and secured by pulling damp brooms across freshly floated or troweled surfaces. Coarse textures suitable for steep slopes (driveways) are produced by stiff-bristle brooms; medium to fine textures are obtained by using soft-bristle brooms. Best results are obtained when using a broom that is specially made for concrete texturing.

A broomed texture can be applied in many ways — in straight lines, curved lines or wavy lines. Driveways, sidewalks and garage floors are usually broomed perpendicular to the direction of traffic.

Curing is one of the most important steps in concrete construction and, according to the Portland Cement Association, one of the most neglected. Proper curing increases the strength and durability of concrete.

The hardening of concrete is brought about by chemical reactions between cement and water. This process, called hydration, continues only if water and a suitable temperature are available. When too much water is lost by evaporation from newly placed concrete, hydration stops. Near freezing temperatures slow hydration almost to a standstill. The purpose of curing is to maintain conditions under which concrete hardens by keeping it moist and warm.

Moist-curing is done in a number of ways: by supplying water with wet coverings or sprinkling to offset the loss of moisture, or by sealing the concrete surface with plastic sheeting, waterproof paper, or curing compounds to prevent the loss of moisture.

Curing should be started as soon as possible so as not to damage the surface. It should continue for a period of five days in warm weather (70 degrees F or 21 C or higher) or seven days in cooler weather (50 to 70 degrees F or 10 to 21 C). The temperature of the concrete must not be allowed to fall below 50 degrees F (10 C) during the curing period.

The first three days are very important in the life of concrete. During this early period, when the cement and water are combining rapidly, the concrete is susceptible to permanent injury. At seven days, the concrete has attained approximately 70 percent strength; at the end of 14 days approximately 85 percent; in 28 days almost full strength. Concrete actually continues to gain strength for years.

An alternate foundation-floor system to that just described eliminates the use of concrete block. This all-poured-concrete method calls for a 12-inch (304.8 mm) wide footing to a depth of 18 inches (457.2 mm) below ground level, a 4-inch (101.6 mm) slab reinforced with 6x6 #10 wire mesh over two inches (50.8 mm) of sand, six mil plastic and 4-inch (101.6 mm) base. Be sure to check with your local building department for footing requirements established in your locale.

The Portland Cement Association recommends use of a foundation or grade beam at the transition point of the garage floor and driveway slabs, or the slabs may be thickened at this point. The floor should be isolated from the foundation wall as shown.

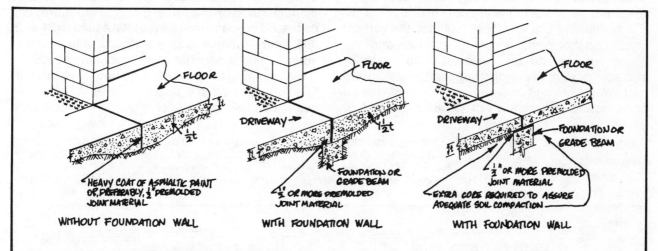

6
Walls

Garage walls are usually frame, cinder block or brick. The selection depends not only on cost, but also on compatibility with the exterior surfaces of the home the garage will serve.

The most popular system, beyond doubt, is wood framing. It is faster to assemble, costs less and provides maximum use of the interior surface.

Wall framing is a term that includes the vertical studs and horizontal members (bottom and top plates, window and door headers) of both exterior and interior walls (if any) that support the ceiling and roof. Wall framing lumber in conventional garage construction is generally 2x4 (38x89 mm) lumber.

The exception is headers over windows and doors in load bearing walls, which may be 2x6's (38x140 mm) or larger, or two or more 2x4's (38x89 mm) nailed together. (Headers span the top of the window or door. Garage door headers can be made sag-proof by using a special header clip. One such device is manufactured by The Panel Clip Co.) Wall studs can be placed on standard 16-inch (406.4 mm) or 24-inch (609.6 mm) module to save materials, if this form of construction is permitted by local building code.

By preparing the concrete slab floor first, this surface provides all the space needed to assemble complete wall sections at ground level and then

Wall framing costs can be reduced by using a 24 inch (609.6 mm) module in planning the garage. These two drawings show a six foot (1.8 meters) wall section not on module (left) and the same-length section on module (right). The later results in 20 percent less vertical framing for the wall. (Drawing courtesy of National Forest Products Association)

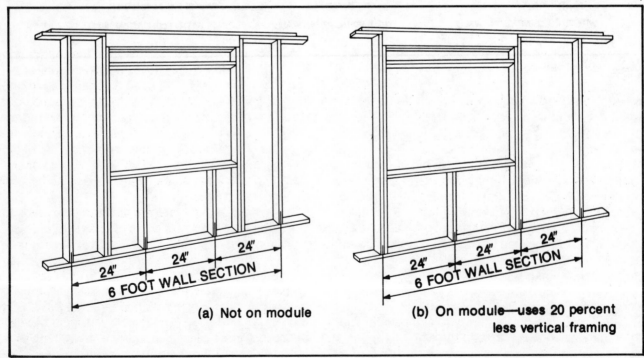

(a) Not on module

(b) On module—uses 20 percent less vertical framing

Garage header clips eliminate the need for a steel flitch plate and costly drilling and bolting. These clips are designed in accordance with accepted engineering standards. (Drawing courtesy of The Panel Clip Co.)

raise them into place. Two persons can usually handle a wall up to 24 feet (7.3 meters) in length, unsheathed. Should sheathing or siding be applied at ground level, mechanical wall jacks can be used to raise the wall.

Treated lumber should be used for the 2x4 (38x89 mm) wood sills, which go around the perimeter of the garage. This wood is drilled to accept the foundation bolts installed in the concrete footings. Usually 5/8-inch (15.8 mm) holes are made in the sill to accept the 1/2-inch (12.7 mm) anchor bolts. Some garage contractors prefer to use a double 2x4 (38x89 mm) sill, setting the bottom layer in sill caulk and using the top member for floor-level assembly of the wall structure. In this way, both sill members are bolted in place with the foundation bolts, with the top sill also nailed to the lower for added strength.

Some local building codes call for the installation of a metal termite shield with the sill. This shield is usually placed between the concrete and the wood sill.

Sill plates should be placed along the foundation and marked for vertical stud location using 16 or 24-inch (406.4 or 609.6 mm) centers, again depending upon local building code. The studs then can be laid out on the floor along with window and door headers, cripple studs (shortened studs) and windowsills. Top plates (sill plates used at the top of the frame) and sill are then nailed to all vertical members and adjoining studs to headers and sills with sixteen penny nails.

A variation of this system is fastening the studs to the top plate only and when the wall is erected, toenailing studs to the sill which has been previously secured to the foundaiton. This technique can be more difficult to do.

After all the walls are erected, a second top plate is added. These members lap adjoining walls at corners to tie all walls together. These top plates also can be partly fastened in place when the wall is in the horizontal position. Top plates are nailed together with sixteen penny nails spaced 16 inches (406.4 mm) apart and with two nails at each wall intersection.

Walls are normally plumbed and aligned before the top plate is added. By using 1x6 (19x140 mm) or 1x8 (19x184 mm) temporary braces on the studs between intersecting partitions, a straight wall is assured. These braces are nailed to the studs at the top of the wall and to a 2x4 (38x89 mm) block fastened to the floor or a stake driven in the ground outside the garage area. The temporary bracing is left in place until the ceiling and roof framing are completed and sheathing is applied to the outside walls.

Wall sheathing is the outside covering used over the wall framework of studs, plates, and window and door headers. It forms the flat base upon which the exterior finish can be applied. Certain types of sheathing and methods of application can provide great rigidity to the house, eliminating the need for corner bracing. Sheathing serves to minimize air infiltration and, in certain forms, can provide some insulation.

SIDING

Some sheet materials serve both as sheathing and siding. Sheathing is sometimes eliminated in the mild climates of the south and west. Likewise, some siding systems for garages do not require building paper (tarpaper) unless called for by the building code.

In selecting siding for the garage, keep in mind its relationship to siding materials used on the home. Most prefer to match the house siding, especially if the garage is to be attached to the house. The siding selected must do justice to the architectural styling of the house and it should be as maintenance-free as possible.

Today you may choose from a number of basic types and styles of siding such as wood and wood-base materials, metal, plastic, masonry and mineral composition. Each has its own characteristics and may be found in most locales. Siding can be obtained in many different patterns and can be stained, painted or finished naturally.

To estimate how much siding is needed to cover the garage walls, first calculate the total surface area. For each exterior wall, multiply the length by the height. To calculate the area of a gable, multiply the length by the height and then divide the result in half. Add these square-footage figures together, plus any "column" siding surfaces across the entry of the garage.

Installation of metal, plastic and mortar siding is accomplished with various types of fastening devices engineered for the respective materials. Wood siding may be applied with corrosion-resistant nails, usually galvanized steel or aluminum. The length of the nail varies with the thickness of the siding and type of sheathing.

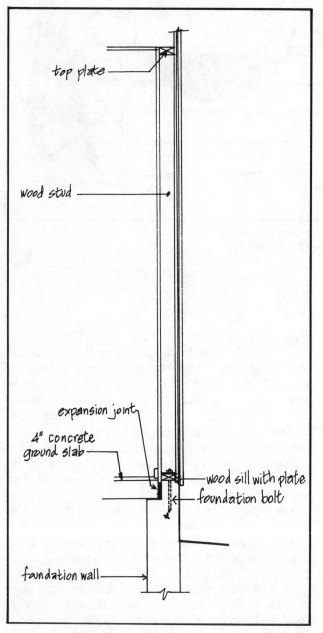

This drawing shows a wood stud bolted to the foundation. (Drawing by Linda A. Zitzewitz)

Labels in drawing: top plate — wood stud — expansion joint — 4" concrete ground slab — wood sill with plate — foundation bolt — foundation wall

Patterns in Plywood Siding

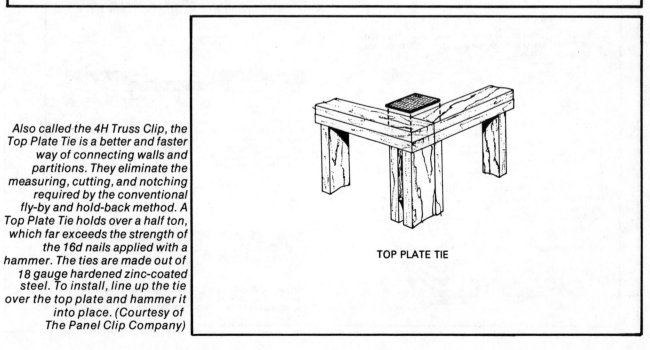

Plain — ⅜" or ⅝" no grooves. Ruf-Sawn redwood has square edges. Ruf-Sawn 316 and Stucco 316 have shiplap edges. Ruf-Sawn fir has square or shiplap edges.

Inverted Batten 12 — ⅝" thick. 1½" wide grooves 12" o.c.

Inverted Batten 8 — ⅝" thick. 1" wide grooves 8" o.c.

Pattern 8 — ⅜" or ⅝" thick. Grooves 8" o.c. ⅜" wide by ¹⁄₁₆" deep (⅜") or ¼" deep (⅝").

Pattern 4 — ⅜" or ⅝" thick. Grooves 4" o.c., ⅜" wide by ¹⁄₁₆" deep (⅜") or ¼" deep (⅝").

Plywood siding panels are produced in various thicknesses as well as face surfaces. (Drawing: Simpson Timber Co.)

Also called the 4H Truss Clip, the Top Plate Tie is a better and faster way of connecting walls and partitions. They eliminate the measuring, cutting, and notching required by the conventional fly-by and hold-back method. A Top Plate Tie holds over a half ton, which far exceeds the strength of the 16d nails applied with a hammer. The ties are made out of 18 gauge hardened zinc-coated steel. To install, line up the tie over the top plate and hammer it into place. (Courtesy of The Panel Clip Company)

TOP PLATE TIE

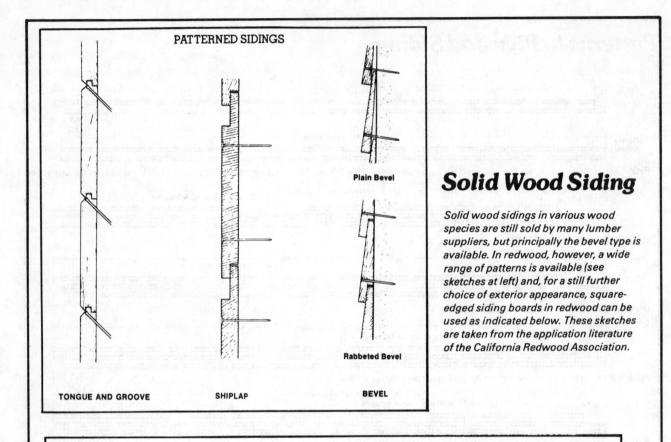

PATTERNED SIDINGS

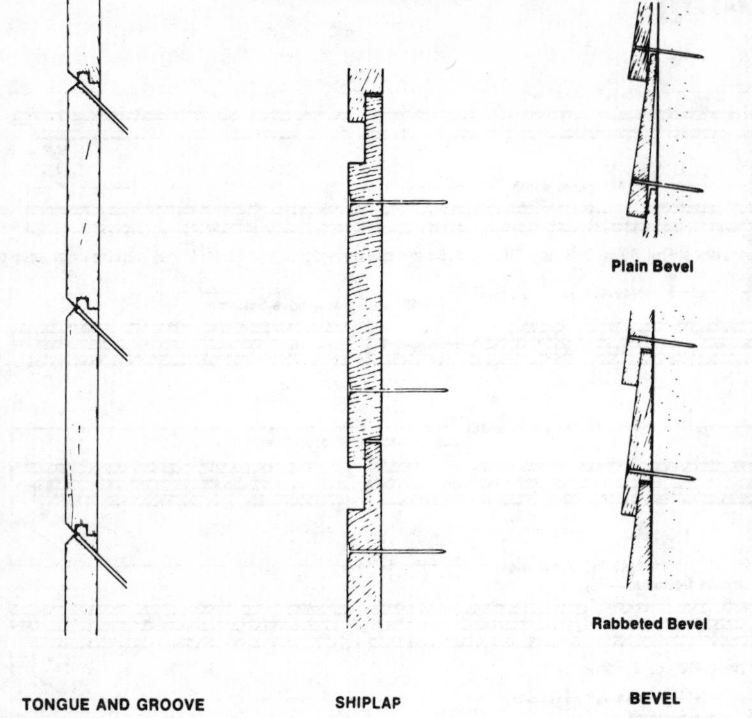
Plain Bevel
Rabbeted Bevel
TONGUE AND GROOVE
SHIPLAP
BEVEL

Solid Wood Siding

Solid wood sidings in various wood species are still sold by many lumber suppliers, but principally the bevel type is available. In redwood, however, a wide range of patterns is available (see sketches at left) and, for a still further choice of exterior appearance, square-edged siding boards in redwood can be used as indicated below. These sketches are taken from the application literature of the California Redwood Association.

BOARD SIDINGS

Nominal and standard dressed sizes for boards, strips, and dimension lumber are shown in the table below.

THICKNESS		WIDTH		
ROUGH (Nominal)	DRESSED S1S or S2S Green or Dry	ROUGH (Nominal)	DRESSED S1E or S2E Green	DRESSED S1E or S2E Dry Finish
¾	11/16	3	2 9/16	2½
1	¾*	4	3 9/16	3½
1¼	1 1/16	6	5⅝	5½
1½	1 5/16	8	7½	7¼
2	1⅝	10	9½	9¼
		12	11½	11¼

*The standard for green 1" is 25/32 but is frequently manufactured to ¾" net.

Vertical grain has greater stability than flat grain, and weathers exceptionally well. It is usually preferred for exterior finish carpentry. Flat grain redwood is highly figured as compared to the more subdued, uniform pattern of vertical grain redwood.

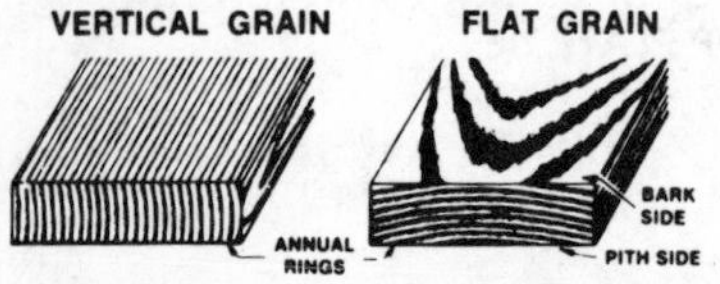
VERTICAL GRAIN
FLAT GRAIN
BARK SIDE
ANNUAL RINGS
PITH SIDE

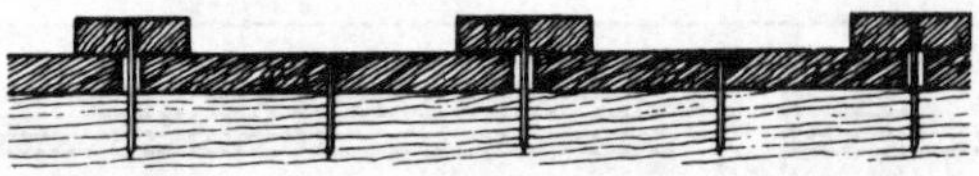

STANDARD BOARD AND BATTEN: Drive one 8d nail midway between edges of the underboard, at each bearing. Then apply batten strips and nail with one 10d nail at each bearing so that shank passes through space between underboards.

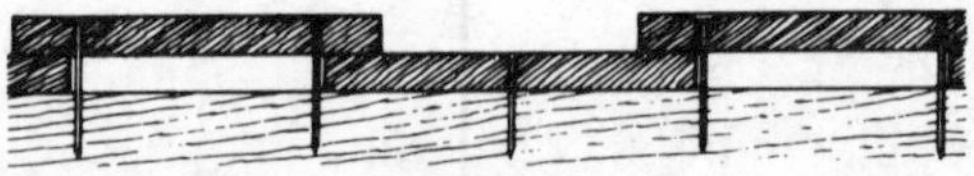

BOARD ON BOARD: Space underboards to allow 1½-inch overlap by outer boards at both edges. Use one 8d nail per bearing for underboards. Outer boards must be nailed twice per bearing to insure proper fastening; use 10d nails, driven so that the shanks clear the underboard by approximately ¼ inch.

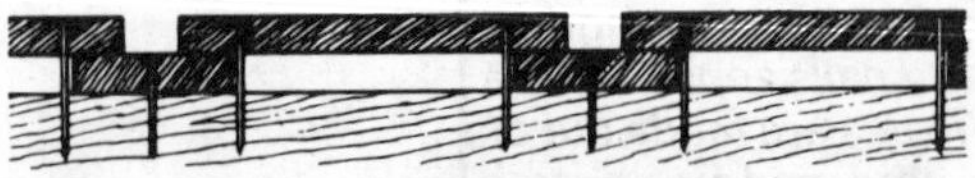

REVERSE BATTEN: Nailing is similar to board on board. Drive one 8d nail per bearing through center of under strip, and two 10d nails per bearing through outer boards.

Here, in alphabetical order, is a rundown on the various types of siding now on the market:

Aluminum

Aluminum siding usually carries a 20-year guarantee against defects (not weathering or fading) and is manufactured in numerous colors, styles and textures for application over sheathing or directly to studs. The lightweight material comes in horizontal patterns and vertical panels with necessary color-matching accessories.

Asbestos

Not as readily available as in past decades, this material is the most easily damaged as it will shatter from a heavy blow. The material comes in both 12x24 (304.8x609.6 mm) shingles and 4-foot (1.2 meters) high and 4 to 12-foot (1.2 to 3.6 meters) long pre-assembled panels. Maintenance is with a garden hose, but the material may be painted.

Cedar Shingles

Cedar shingles and shakes (shingles are smooth, shakes have grooved texture) are sold in 25 square foot (2.3 square meters) bundles. There are two basic methods of shingle wall application: single-coursed and double-coursed. In single-course construction, weather exposures are employed which are slightly less than one-half the nominal shingle length. They are as follows: 16-inch (406.4 mm) length exposure — 7-1/2 inches (190.5 mm); 18-inch (457.2 mm) length exposure — 8-1/2 inches (215.9 mm); 24-inch (609.6 mm) exposure — 11-1/2 inches (292.1 mm).

In double coursing, two layers of shingles — one directly over the other — are applied. The top course, machine grooved shakes or shingles, normally are of No. 1 grade with lower grades used for the inner and completely concealed layer. With the doubled courses, extended weather exposures are permissible: 16-inch (406.4 mm) length — 12-inch (304.8 mm) exposure; 18-inch (457.2 mm) length — 14-inch (355.6 mm) exposure; 24-inch (609.6 mm) length — 16-inch (406.4 mm) exposure.

Several nailing methods may be used to apply shingles to side walls. On solid sheathing, the shingles are applied directly over a good grade building paper. On open sheathing (2x4 or 38x89 mm vertical studs), paper is applied over the studs and 1x4 (19x89 mm) nailing strips spaced so the course lines fall two inches (50.8 mm) below strip centers.

Grooved sidewall shakes, aside from being available in natural color, are offered in either prime-coated or finish-coated in a wide range of colors. Where the building code permits, 8-foot (2.4 meters) shingle and shake panels (plain or colored) may be nailed directly to studs on 16- or 24-inch (406.4 or 609.6 mm) centers.

Hardboard

Hardboard is a long-lasting material that is seldom damaged. This exterior siding comes in many finishes and styles to simulate rustic planks, clapboard, board-and-batten, contemporary V-groove paneling and stucco surfaces. Some hardboards are preprimed while others are prefinished. Hardboard has no knots or grain to rise and check, and it doesn't splinter, split or crack. It is easy to work with using standard carpenter tools.

Hardboard may be applied over sheathed or unsheathed walls, and generally holds paint longer than lumber sidings. Hardboard lap siding is 7/16-inches (11 mm) thick (nominal) and comes in 16-foot (4.8 meters) lengths. Widths range from 6 to 12 inches (152.4 to 304.8 mm). Panels for vertical application are four feet (1.2 meters) wide and 8, 9 or 10-feet (2.4, 2.7 or 3 meters) long. Thickness is 7/16 inches (11 mm), nominal. These panels come in a variety of grooved patterns — and frequently are used with battens.

Plywood

Plywood siding offers a great range of sidewall surfacing treatments. Wood species such as redwood, fir, cypress and cedar are used in the manufacture of various overlaid, grooved and textured plywoods, some of which are factory-primed and others which are factory-finished.

There are over a dozen general types of plywood sidings, including self-aligning lap and the many vertical panel types. Groovings range all the way from wide 1-1/2-inch (38.1 mm) furrowed grooves that are 12 or 16 inches (304.8 or 406.4 mm) on center (reverse board and batten), to the popular Texture 1-11 type and other grooves two, four, six, eight or 16-inches (50.8, 101.6, 152.4, 203.2 or 406.4 mm) on center. There also is narrow saw kerfing. Most types of panels have shiplapped or tongue-and-groove edge choices. All standard plywood siding thicknesses are represented.

Plywood surfaces range all the way from sanded to rough sawn, striated or brushed, and in various grades including such faces as knotty cedar. There are medium density overlaid surfaces, paint-primed and even acrylic-overlaid permanent colors.

Lap siding comes in various plywood lengths up to 16 feet (4.8 meters) with one-piece overlaid faces. Vertical plywood sidings are generally available in 4-foot (1.2 meters) widths, and up to 10-foot (3 meters) lengths. Some come up to 12 feet (3.6 meters), and a few to 16 feet (4.8 meters).

Redwood

Redwood is a widely-used, all-weather siding available in a broad range of attractive grades, patterns and sizes. A choice of rough-sawn or smooth textures enhances the pleasing contrasts of deep red heartwood and creamy sapwood. Even construction grades are frequently chosen for highly visible applications.

The California Redwood Association and most manufacturers recommend clear all heart and clear grades for siding applications, and stress that both should be "Certified Kiln Dried" or bear the initials "CKD." Also recommended is preapplication treatment with a water repellent, which will improve the finish performance no matter what type of finish is used.

Among the styles of redwood siding currently offered are plain bevel, rabbeted bevel, shiplap, V rustic, tongue and groove, channel rustic, and board and batten. This highly insulative material can be ordered with factory-applied water repellent, primed with paint, or finished with stain. No other commercial softwood product takes and holds stain or paint better than redwood. Yet without a finish, redwood performs equally well and with the seasons its deep reddish-brown coloring turns gradually to a silvery driftwood gray.

Steel

Steel siding is a highly sophisticated product, most often applied by a professional contractor. The product is offered in many different colors achieved with silicone resins and color pigments. These coatings provide chalk resistance, gloss and color retention, and resistance to erosion and abrasion. Standard styles include clapboard and vertical panels, plus a full range of accessory items including gutters, downspouts, soffit and fascia trim.

Solid Vinyl

Solid vinyl sidewall covering combines acoustical and thermal insulation properties with the aesthetic appeal of natural wood. The siding has the look of painted wood, yet requires little or no maintenance and painting since the color runs throughout the material. It is impervious to pollutants in the air, and unaffected by fungi and termites.

Solid vinyl siding comes in an embossed wood grain texture or smooth finish, in a choice of colors including gold, yellow, white, green, gray, and others. Both clapboard and vertical-panel styles are offered, along with a full line of accessories including gutter and soffit systems. The material is applied with standard carpenter tools.

Wood

Wood siding comes in the widest range of patterns, installation styles and textures. The material is clear or knotty, rough-sawn or smooth. Its beauty can be enriched and protected by oils, deepened by stains, or painted for special effects.

All wood siding and exterior trim should be thoroughly dry when installed, and free of dampness or moisture condensation when painted. Most firms offer wood siding that has been water-repellent treated, or paint-primed on the back or both surfaces. Such applications are beneficial in protecting the siding from any later effects from adverse moisture conditions.

Preprimed siding, also available, has a complete prime coat on the siding face, as well as a protective prime or treatment on the reverse side. This provides a superior base for additional coats of quality paint.

CONCRETE BLOCKS & BRICK

Concrete blocks also can be used for walls. They are available in various sizes and forms, but those generally used are eight, 10 and 12 inches (203.2, 254, and 304.8 mm) wide. Modular blocks allow for the thickness and width of the mortar joint so are usually about 7-5/8-inches (193.75 mm) high by 15-5/8-inches (396.8 mm) long. This results in blocks that measure eight inches (200 mm) high and 16 inches (400 mm) long from centerline to centerline of the mortar joints.

Concrete block walls require no form work. Block courses (each row of blocks) start at the footing and

Walls laid in a running bond pattern are the simplest to construct. It is one of the most common patterns used.

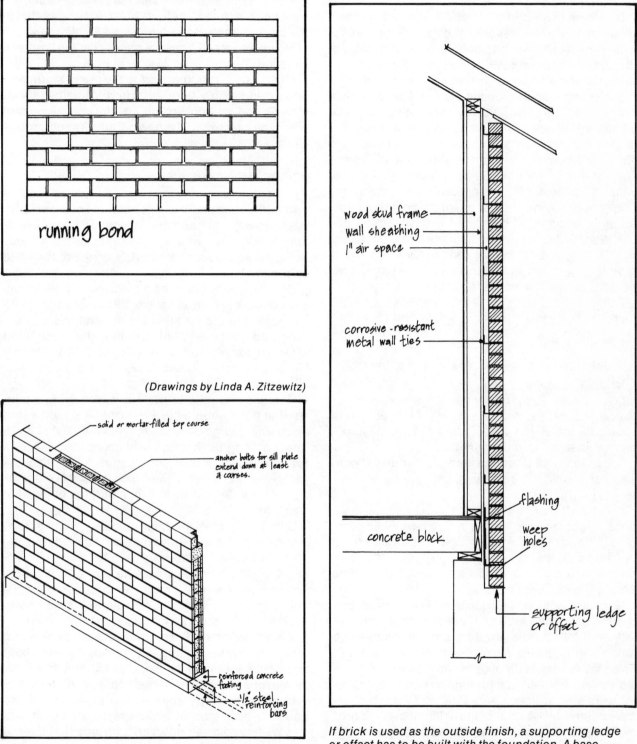

running bond

(Drawings by Linda A. Zitzewitz)

solid or mortar-filled top course

anchor bolts for sill plate extend down at least 2 courses.

reinforced concrete footing

1/2" steel reinforcing bars

The top course of a concrete block wall is filled with mortar. Anchor bolts are placed through the top two rows of blocks.

wood stud frame
wall sheathing
1" air space

corrosive-resistant metal wall ties

flashing

concrete block

weep holes

supporting ledge or offset

If brick is used as the outside finish, a supporting ledge or offset has to be built with the foundation. A base flashing and weep holes help protect the construction from moisture. Corrosive-resistant metal wall ties bond the brick to the framework.

are laid up with about 3/8-inch (9.5 mm) mortar joints, usually in a running bond. Joints should be tooled smooth to resist water seepage. A full bedding of mortar should be used on all contact surfaces of the block.

Block walls should be capped with four inches (101.6 mm) of solid masonry or concrete reinforced with wire mesh. Anchor bolts are usually placed through the top two rows of blocks and the top cap to accept the wood plate for securing roof framing.

If masonry veneer is used for the outside finish over wood-frame walls, the foundation must include a supporting ledge or offset about five inches (127 mm) wide. This results in a space of about one inch (25.4 mm) between the masonry and sheathing for ease of laying the brick. A base flashing (material which gives protection from moisture) is used at the brick course below the bottom of the sheathing and framing, and should be lapped with sheathing paper. Weep holes to provide drainage also are located in this course and are formed by eliminating the mortar in a vertical joint. Of course, these steps must be done before the walls are put up.

Corrosion-resistant metal ties — spaced about 32 inches (812.8 mm) apart horizontally and 16 inches (406.4 mm) vertically — should be used to bond the brick veneer to the framework. Where other than wood sheathing is used, secure the ties to the studs.

Brick and stone should be laid in a full bed of mortar; avoid dropping mortar into the space between the veneer and sheathing. Outside joints should be tooled to a smooth finish to get the maximum resistance to water penetration.

Keep in mind that masonry laid during cold weather should be protected from freezing until after the mortar has set.

If desired, the inside garage walls can be lined once ceiling and roof construction have been completed. Various panel materials are offered at retail building material outlets, including perforated hardboards which turn the walls into complete storage units. (See chapter on Storage.)

Gypsum wallboard also may be used (install any desired insulation first) and is best applied horizontally to minimize the lineal footage of joints to be taped and finished. When this material is used to finish the garage ceiling, panels may be applied horizontally (perpendicular to joists) or vertically (parallel to joists), whichever method will result in the fewest joints. Use the longest lengths of boards available. Butt joints, if any, should be staggered.

Most garages are unheated, but those in colder climates can be made more comfortable for workshop projects through the addition of wall and ceil-

ing insulation. Full-thick insulation (3-5/8 inches or 92 mm) installed in frame walls comes in easy-to-handle batts which have stapling edges for quick, permanent location.

Those garages with finished ceilings, (as opposed to open roof truss construction), can be insulated in the same manner or with loose fill insulation which is blown into place once the garage ceiling has been installed.

Most insulation experts urge the use of storm windows and flexible door-surround insulation ahead of wall and ceiling insulation of garages, except when the space over the new garage is to be used as a living area.

DOORS AND WINDOWS

In addition to the main garage door (detailed on later pages), one pedestrian or service door is recommended. This unit should be installed at floor level to permit access without using the automobile entrance.

Service doors are widely available as packaged units complete with all necessary framing and prefitted hardware. You merely set the unit in place between the prepared stud opening, shim (use filler) where necessary and nail in place. A 2-foot 6-inch x 6-foot 8-inch (.6 meters, 152.4 mm x 1.8 meters, 203.2 mm) unit usually is sufficient.

Garages attached to the home, requiring a connecting door, should have this door installed a step above the garage floor to help prevent dust and dirt from entering the home. Local codes also call for a fire-type (solid) door in this location. In addition, the garage wall adjoining the home must have a one-hour or greater fire rating via a surface of gypsum wallboard.

Garage windows are most desirable if the garage is to be used for any other purpose beyond housing the automobile. Window styles in the home will dictate the type and influence the size and location. Some homeowners prefer fixed windows while others prefer a window with screen so summer breezes may reduce heat buildup in the garages.

It is better to have the service door and window on the left wall of the garage as they provide better light and easier access to the driver's seat. But there may be reasons for wanting these openings on the other wall of the garage, such as easier access to the house, service yard or breezeway. Then again, you may wish to have windows on both sides to increase the natural lighting. A window or door also could be installed in the rear wall, but doing so generally takes away from valuable wall storage space.

7
Roofs

There are many different types of roofs suitable to garage construction (see Chapter 1), but above all else, the one you choose should harmonize with your house. Here are a few other considerations, by type:

Gable — fairly simple to construct and provides the greatest amount of storage space.

Flat — even easier to build and saves on roofing materials. May permit a sun deck or play space on top of the garage, but allows little storage space and supporting beams must be heavier. Built-up roofing materials must be used.

Hip — more difficult to build, yet often attractive. All four sides slope down from the ridge, typical of French Provincial architecture.

Shed — very popular in garages built during the 1930's and 40's. Consists of one straight plane, much in keeping with contemporary architectural designs. Can provide overhead protection at front of garage.

Mansard — dresses up a flat-top type design and provides some overhead storage space. Especially popular in townhouse-style residences.

Gambrel — looks somewhat like a gable roof folded down once on each side. Of Dutch origin, this style has been widely used for barn construction and provides overhead storage area.

TRUSSES

Whether the garage roof is conventionally built or engineered with prefabricated trusses, its structure is formed with lumber in almost every instance. Unlike construction of the balance of the house, the

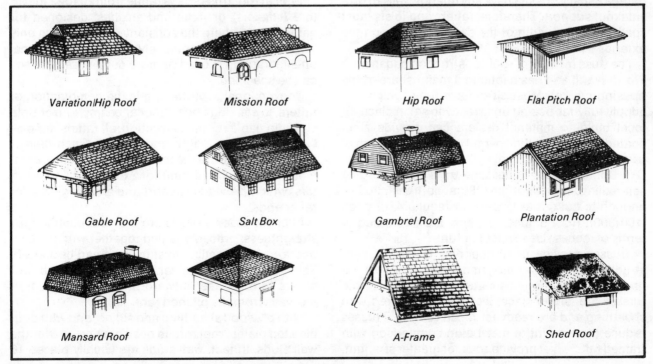

Variation/Hip Roof   Mission Roof   Hip Roof   Flat Pitch Roof

Gable Roof   Salt Box   Gambrel Roof   Plantation Roof

Mansard Roof   A-Frame   Shed Roof

Reprinted, by permission, from Schram, *Improving the Outside of Your Home.*

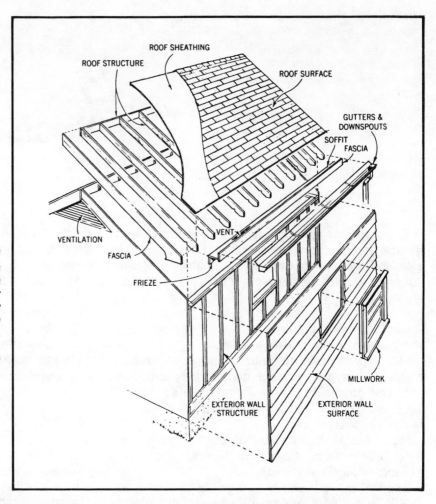

Components of garage roof construction are illustrated in this cut-away drawing. Various materials may be selected for finish surfaces, but the assembly system remains basically the same as detailed in this chapter. (Drawing courtesy of U.S. Gypsum Co.)

garage usually doesn't have any interior walls to provide roof support. Therefore, rafters and joists must span the entire width of the garage, resting on the exterior walls.

The truss method of roof construction began after World War II and has captured a major share of the housing market. Most cities have firms which can supply fully-fabricated units ready to set in place, or local building material dealers can provide zinc-coated steel clips which permit on-site fabrication of trusses with conventional tools. One firm, The Panel Clip Co., offers stock package units containing 64 self-nailing, high-strength, 18-gauge truss clips — enough to build four trusses for regular 4/12 pitch (100/300). Roof slopes, or pitch, are expressed in terms of inches rise to a foot of run.

Trusses provide great economy in garage construction for they permit complete assembly of the garage roof framing in a matter of hours. Once the trusses are laid in place, they can be covered with sheathing and are ready for finish roofing. Trusses reduce the amount of material in comparison with framed rafters, yet provide equal or greater strength.

Typical roof truss spans range from 20 to 32 feet (6 to 9.7 meters) or more and are best designed for garage roofs where the constant width requires only one type of truss. For other style roofs, conventional on-site framing is used or more customized trusses can be specified.

Conventional roof framing is the combination of rafters, joists, ridge board, collar beams, and cripple studs. In gable roof construction, all rafters are pre-cut to the same length and pattern. Each pair of rafters is fastened at the top to the ridge board, commonly a 2x8 (38x184 mm) for 2x6 (38x140 mm) rafters, which provides support and a nailing area for rafter ends.

After the exterior walls are erected, plumbed for straightness, braced and tied together with the second top plates, ceiling joist framing can be started. This framing ties together opposite walls and roof rafters to resist the outward pressure imposed on the walls from the pitched roof.

With plywood sheathing and siding, and with doubled top plates, roof rafters need not line up over the wall studs. In fact, wall studs are usually placed 16 inches (406.4 mm) on center, whereas roof rafters can be placed at 24 inches (609.6 mm) on center.

Hip roofs are framed the same as a gable roof at the center section of a rectangular garage. The ends are framed with hip rafters which extend from each outside corner of the wall to the ridge board at a 45 degree angle. Jack rafters extend from the top plates to the hip rafters.

When roof spans are long and slopes are flat, it is common practice to use collar beams between opposing rafters. Steeper slopes and shorter spans also may require collar beams but only on every third rafter. Collar beams may be 1x6 (19x140 mm) material.

In low-slope roof designs, the style of architecture often dictates the use of a ridge beam. These solid, glu-laminated or nail-laminated beams span the open area and are usually supported by an exterior wall at both ends, or by an exterior wall at one end and an interior partition wall or a post at the other when the garage is attached to the house.

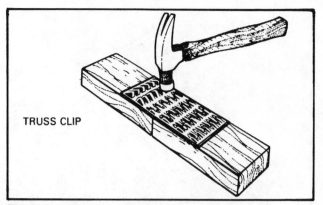

The most versatile selection of Truss Clips on the market are manufactured by the Panel Clip Company. They are made of 18 gauge, quarter hard, zinc-coated steel. Available in eleven sizes, Truss Clips can be installed quickly by hand with a hammer or with a high-speed Truss Press. Truss Clips are accepted by FHA and other building codes. Their holding power is 50 lbs. per tooth. (Drawing courtesy of The Panel Clip Company)

Roof slopes portrayed in this sketch indicate the suitability of asphalt shingles for various slope conditions. Rise, run and pitch are common terms used when discussing roof slopes. And it is common practice to describe a slope or pitch in rise-to-run figures, such as "3-in-12".

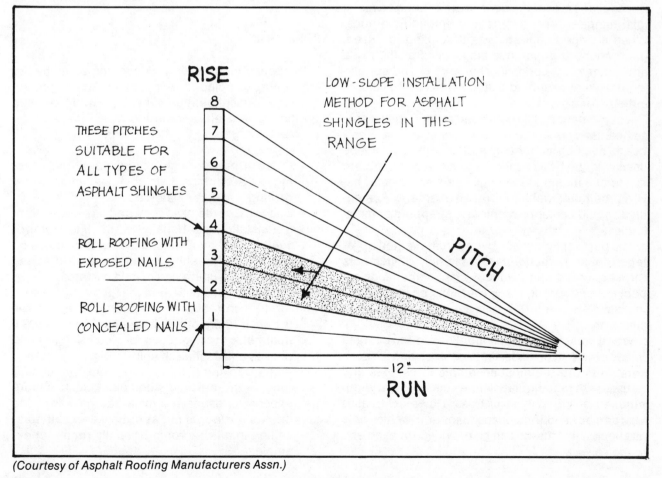

(Courtesy of Asphalt Roofing Manufacturers Assn.)

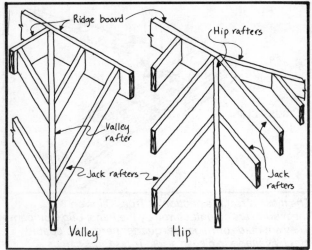

Valley and hip framing is the most difficult part of rafter framing work done at the site. They require precision measuring and cutting on complex angles. Most roof truss fabricators are now capable of prefabricating truss components that assemble at the site to form hipped roofs and eliminate the need for precision on-site cutting. (Courtesy Successful How to Build Your Own Home, by Robert C. Reschke)

The beam must be designed to support the roof load for the span selected. Wood decking (solid planks) can serve both as supporting and sheathing. Spaced rafters over the ridge beam or hung on metal joist hangers serve as alternate framing methods. When a ridge beam and wood decking are used, good anchoring methods are needed at the ridge and outer wall. Long ringshank nails and supplemental metal strapping or angle iron can be used at both bearing areas.

A combination of large spaced rafters which serve as beams for longitudinal wood or structural fiberboard decking is another system which might be used with the ridge beam. Rafters can be supported by metal hangers at the ridge beam and extend beyond the outer walls to form an overhang. Fastenings should be supplemented by strapping or metal angles.

The popular lightweight wood truss method of garage roof construction is an assembly of members forming a rigid framework of triangular shapes capable of supporting loads over long spans without intermediate support. This is a must in garage construction.

Wood trusses most commonly used for garages include the W-type truss, the King-post, and the scissors. They are the most adaptable to garages and houses with rectangular plans — the constant width requires only one type of truss. However, trusses also can be used for L-shape plans and for hip roofs as special hip trusses can be provided for each end of the valley area.

Trusses are commonly designed for two-foot (.6 meters) spacing. This requires somewhat thicker interior and exterior sheathing or finish material than is needed for conventional joist and rafter construction using 16-inch (406.4 mm) spacing. Truss designs, lumber grades and construction details are available through local building material dealers.

The design of the truss not only includes snow and windload considerations, but the weight of the roof itself. Design also takes into account the slope of the roof. Generally, the flatter the slope, the greater the stresses. This results not only in the need for larger members, but also in stronger connections. Consequently, all conditions must be considered before the type of truss is selected and designed.

An important detail in erecting trusses is the method of anchoring. Because of their single member thickness, it is usually desirable to use some type of metal connector to supplement toenailing at the wallplates. Plate anchors are available commercially and provide a resistance to uplift stresses. Many dealers supply trusses with a 2x4 (38x89 mm) soffit return at the end of each upper chord to provide nailing areas for the soffit.

SHEATHING

Roof sheathing will vary, depending upon the finish roofing selected for the garage. Here again, the finish material should be in keeping with that used on the home itself. Among the types of sheathing used are:

- **Closed Boards** which are applied without spacing to accept asphalt shingles, metal-sheet roofing and other materials.
- **Spaced Boards** used for wood shake and shingle installations. Usually 1x3's (19x64 mm) or 1x4's (19x89 mm) spaced the same distance on centers as the shingles are to be laid to the weather. (Usually used in mild climates.)
- **Plywood,** usually 5/16-inch (7.9 mm) thickness for 16-inch (406.4 mm) spacing of rafters and 3/8-inch (9.5 mm) thickness for 24-inch (609.6 mm) rafter spacing. Used for wood shingles and shakes and asphalt shingles.
- **Plank Decking** of 2-inch (50.8 mm) and thicker tongue-and-grooved wood planking. It is more expensive, especially for a garage where the interior surface is not as critical as a cathedral ceiling in a living room or family room, for example.

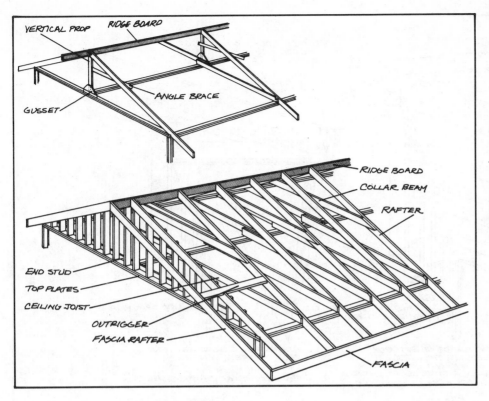

Garage roof framing can be accomplished piece by piece or can utilize factory-made (or job-site fabricated) trusses. This drawing details standard framing members and their placement in a conventional roof structure. (Drawing courtesy of American Plywood Association)

- **Fiberboard Decking** comes in thicknesses ranging from 1-1/2 to 3 inches (38.1 to 76.2 mm), much like wood decking. This material (or wood) is normally used for flat and low-pitched roofs using built-up finish (several layers) roofing systems.

The choice of finish roofing materials is usually influenced by cost, local code requirements, house design, climate, or preferences based upon past experience. Those materials used for pitched garage roofs are wood, asphalt, tile, slate and asbestos shingles. Sheet materials such as roll roofing, galvanized iron, aluminum, copper and tin also are used.

Roof underlay material usually consists of 15 or 30-pound asphalt-saturated felt and should be used in moderate and lower slope roofs covered with asphalt, asbestos or slate shingles, or tile roofing. It is not commonly used for wood shingles and shakes.

Metal roofs are sometimes used on flat decks. Joints should be watertight and the deck properly flashed at the juncture with the house. Nails should be of the same metal as that used on the roof, except with tin roofs, where steel nails may be used. All exposed nail heads in tin roofs should be soldered with a resin-core solder or caulked to prevent water from going down the nail hole.

Built-up roof coverings are installed by roofing companies that specialize in this work. Roofs of this type may have three, four or five layers of roofer's felt, each mopped down with asphalt or tar. The final surface is coated with asphalt and covered with gravel embedded in asphalt or tar, or covered with a cap sheet which eliminates the need to apply further asphalt. For convenience, it is customary to refer to built-up roofs as 10, 15 or 20-year roofs, depending upon the application.

Asphalt shingles today are used on more than 80 percent of homes and garages in the United States, generally for roofs with slopes of 4 inches (101.6 mm) or more per horizontal slope. These shingles come in a variety of styles, the most popular being the square butt strip shingle, elongated in shape and available with three tabs, two tabs or one tab (no cutouts).

Asphalt shingles get their color from the ceramic-coated mineral granules that are embedded in the shingles. These coarse granules also contribute to the shingles' ability to resist fire. Asphalt shingles that bear the Underwriters' Laboratories (UL) label for Class C fire resistance have been tested to assure they will not readily ignite or contribute to the spread of flame. Shingles rated Class B or A afford even better fire protection.

49

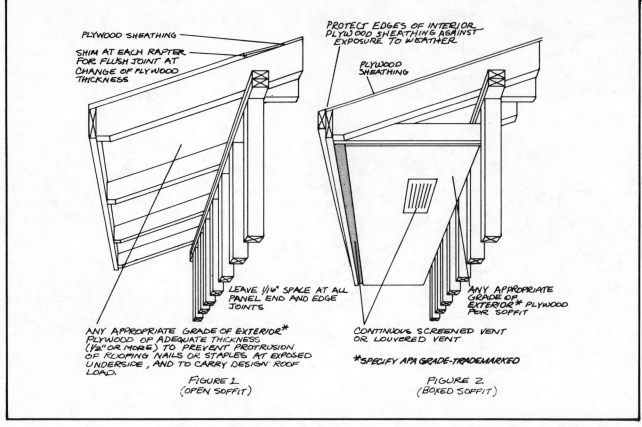

PLYWOOD SHEATHING

SHIM AT EACH RAFTER FOR FLUSH JOINT AT CHANGE OF PLYWOOD THICKNESS

PROTECT EDGES OF INTERIOR PLYWOOD SHEATHING AGAINST EXPOSURE TO WEATHER

PLYWOOD SHEATHING

LEAVE 1/16" SPACE AT ALL PANEL END AND EDGE JOINTS

ANY APPROPRIATE GRADE OF EXTERIOR* PLYWOOD OF ADEQUATE THICKNESS (1/2" OR MORE) TO PREVENT PROTRUSION OF ROOFING NAILS OR STAPLES AT EXPOSED UNDERSIDE, AND TO CARRY DESIGN ROOF LOAD.

FIGURE 1 (OPEN SOFFIT)

CONTINUOUS SCREENED VENT OR LOUVERED VENT

ANY APPROPRIATE GRADE OF EXTERIOR* PLYWOOD FOR SOFFIT

*SPECIFY APA GRADE-TRADEMARKED

FIGURE 2 (BOXED SOFFIT)

Plywood roof sheathing is widely used for garage roof construction to provide structural strength and a solid base for fastening finish roofing materials. These drawings show how the material is extended to form the overhang which can remain open or be finished with a ventilated plywood soffit. (Drawings courtesy of American Plywood Association)

The trend in recent years has been toward heavier shingle weights. For many years the standard, widely used weight of shingle coverage was in the range of 210-240 pounds per hundred square feet. But in recent years new manufacturing methods, plus double-layering and use of larger and heavier granules, have run shingle weight to 300 pounds and more. This better quality, of course, has resulted in higher shingle prices.

Asphalt shingles generally measure 1x3 feet (.3x.9 meters) and it is recommended you use units offering a "seal-tab" provision for maximum wind protection. This feature incorporates a single row of adhesive spots into the shingle at certain locations. Under the heat of the sun the spots soften, and the tabs of the row above settle into the softening adhesive to give an effective protection against wind lifting the tabs.

Normally, for standard size strip shingles, the overlap of one strip to the one below is designed to leave an exposure of 5 inches (127 mm). This provides double coverage, placing at least two layers of basic roofing material at every point of the roof.

Wood shingles and shakes made from cedar and other durable wood species are highly attractive and very popular in many areas of the country. Here again, if these have been used on the house, they should be your first selection for the new garage to maintain the architectural integrity.

Wood shingles and shakes may be laid on slopes as gentle as one in four, but they perform best on steeper slopes. The wood may be stained or left natural, and some are offered prestained. This may be installed over a solid roof sheathing or with slats that allow air flow from the inside garage roof space.

Ceramic, clay and concrete tile roofing is manufactured in flat, rectangular units as well as special shapes for minimum roof pitches of four inches per foot (100/300). With integral color, this type roofing has an indefinite life expectancy. Tile is applied over a solid decking covered with felt and may require additional framing. Tile roofs are rated Class A when it comes to fire resistance. Slate roofing is applied in the same manner as tile, has long life expectancy and shows the grain and texture of stone. This roofing material is among the most costly.

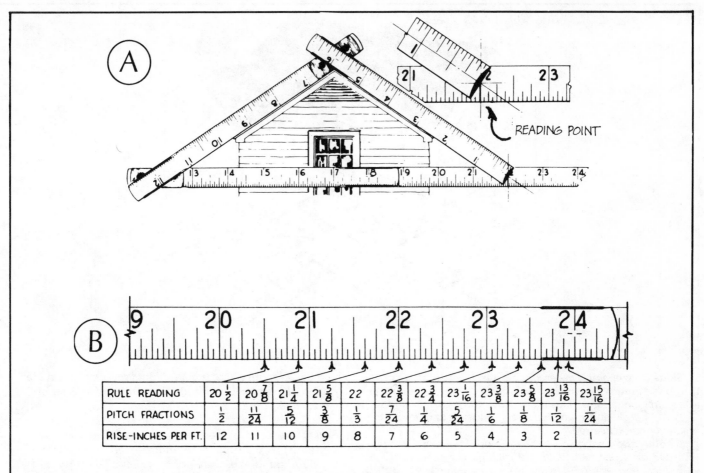

RULE READING	$20\frac{1}{2}$	$20\frac{7}{8}$	$21\frac{1}{4}$	$21\frac{5}{8}$	22	$22\frac{3}{8}$	$22\frac{3}{4}$	$23\frac{1}{16}$	$23\frac{3}{8}$	$23\frac{5}{8}$	$23\frac{13}{16}$	$23\frac{15}{16}$
PITCH FRACTIONS	$\frac{1}{2}$	$\frac{11}{24}$	$\frac{5}{12}$	$\frac{3}{8}$	$\frac{1}{3}$	$\frac{7}{24}$	$\frac{1}{4}$	$\frac{5}{24}$	$\frac{1}{6}$	$\frac{1}{8}$	$\frac{1}{12}$	$\frac{1}{24}$
RISE-INCHES PER FT.	12	11	10	9	8	7	6	5	4	3	2	1

How to Estimate Quantities of Roofing

Computation of the roof area that needs covering is simple when you have a simple floor plan and uncomplicated roof. However, the method given here is suitable for all kinds of homes and roofs. It is the estimating procedure recommended in the application manual issued by the Asphalt Roofing Manufacturers Association. While the procedure may take longer than other estimating methods, it is accurate and allows an estimate from the ground without any roof climbing or roof measuring.

The method converts the house area at ground level to roof area, using conversion factors that depend upon the slope or pitch of the roof. First comes the determination of this slope or slopes. The span, rise and run of a roof can be represented by triangles. In an equilateral (all sides equal) triangle, the base leg represents the span, the height of the triangle represents the rise of the roof, the equilateral legs represent the roof slopes or pitch, and half the base leg or span is what is referred to as "run."

For estimating purposes, the roof pitch or slope angle can be "measured" quite accurately using a carpenter's folding rule as shown in the drawing. One end of the rule is shaped into a triangle while standing away from the home. The rule is held at arm's length and the last two rule sections adjusted to parallel the roof slopes as indicated.

When the two sections have been adjusted so the view shows their angle is parallel to the two roof slopes, hold the overlapping end of the rule firmly on the base section. The reading point is shown by the arrow, sketch A. The reading is taken at the nearest eighth-inch point on the base section, as indicated in sketch B. From that eighth mark go down in the chart below to find the pitch fraction and the rise in inches per horizontal foot. Example: an end-of-the-rule reading of 23⅜ inches means the roof slope has a 4-in-12 pitch.

Ground Area of Home is determined by on-ground measurements using a steel tape. The drawing on the facing page will be used as an example for the balance of the computations. This might be a typical dwelling with a few roof complications in the form of overhangs and dormers, plus ridges at varying heights. The projection below the perspective drawing shows the total ground area covered. In making the roof area computations, exterior wall measurements are taken at ground level but dormer and chimney measurements can be made in the attic space. Most dwellings can be measured up in this manner without need for climbing on the roof. After all measurements have been made and duly noted on paper along with a rough sketch and after the various roof pitches have been determined, you can proceed with the calculation of the different roof portions.

In the example home, the likely starting point is the main roof, whose slope is 9-in-12. This will be followed by the 6-in-12 portion. Then, allowances are made for the duplicated roof areas and for such additions or subtractions as those for chimneys and dormers.

(Courtesy of the Asphalt Roofing Manufacturer's Association)

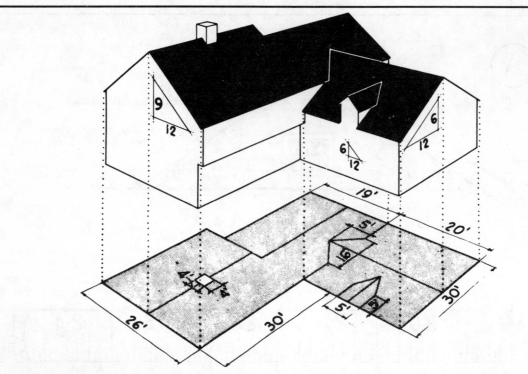

Slope Conversion is necessary because the roof area over a ground area is larger than the ground area. A one-plus conversion factor for various roof pitches can be calculated so that a simple multiplication changes the ground area into the roof area desired.

Later, after roof area has been determined, it will also be necessary to estimate the length of hips, ridges and valleys. Ridges, being parallel to the ground are no problem. But hips and valleys also slope, and need conversion.

The conversion figures below provide factors for more common roof slopes. The horizontal ground area or distance is measured or estimated in square feet or length in feet; multiply that by the conversion factor for the appropriate roof pitch and you come up with the roof area or hip/valley length.

Adjustments to roof area calculations are needed for supplementary areas such as the single dormer in the example house or places where one roof area may project over another because of eave overhangs. There are also adjustments to be made where the overhangs, eave or rake, extend beyond exterior walls. Even a short overhang can mean a substantial area to be added with some homes.

In the example drawing, just a 4-inch eave overhang with duplications accounted for will add about 12 square feet of area for the duplicated portions, before conversion to roof area. After all roof areas have been calculated and the summation made to reach a total area, add about 10 percent more area to cover wasted material. Roofing shingles are

sold by the square, that is per hundred square feet. Divide your total area by 100 to obtain the number of squares of material required.

Accessories need to be estimated in much the same way, beginning with the hip-valley-ridge lengths needed for hip-ridge shingles or flashings for valleys. Eave and rake lengths will be added to give the total lengths needed of metal edging. The amounts of nails and roofing cement required will depend upon the nature of the job, rather than the areas. Obtain guidance from your roofing supplier at the time that materials are ordered.

CONVERSION TABLE		
Pitch Rise	Roof Area Factor	Hip/Valley Factor
4 inches per foot	1.054	1.452
5 " " "	1.083	1.474
6 " " "	1.118	1.500
7 " " "	1.157	1.524
8 " " "	1.202	1.564
9 " " "	1.250	1.600
10 " " "	1.302	1.642
11 " " "	1.356	1.684
12 " " "	1.414	1.732

FLASHINGS, GUTTERS & DOWNSPOUTS

Sheet metal work involved in garage and carport construction normally consists of flashing, gutters and downspouts, and sometimes ventilators.

Flashing should be used at the junction of a roof and a wood or masonry wall, over exposed doors and windows, at siding material changes, in roof valleys, and other areas where rain or snow may penetrate into the garage or house. Flashing also is

Ridge shingles are single-tab widths cut from shingle strips and applied with same exposure as used with the field shingles. Use one nail each side of the ridge. With hands, carefully pre-bend each ridge shingle. In some areas, suppliers offer pre-cut ridge and hip shingles.

(Courtesy How to Build Your Own Home, by Robert C. Reschke)

required at the junctions of an exterior wall and a flat or low-pitched built-up roof. Stack vents and roof ventilators are provided with flashing collars which are lapped by the shingles on the upper side. The lower edge of the collar laps the shingles. Sides are nailed to the shingles and caulked with roofing mastic, a pastelike cement.

Several types of gutters are available to guide the rainwater to the downspouts and away from the foundation. Perhaps the most commonly used gutter is the type hung from the edge of the roof or fastened to the edge of the cornice fascia. Metal gutters may be half round or the formed type and may be galvanized metal, copper or aluminum. Some have factory-applied enamel finish. Plastic gutters and downspouts also are available.

On flat roofs, water is drained from one or more locations and carried through an inside wall to an underground drain. All downspouts connected to an underground drain should contain basket strainers at the junction of the gutter to prevent leaves or twigs from going into the drain. This system is installed before the roof is attached.

Downspouts are round or rectangular, the round type being used for the half-round gutters. They are usually corrugated to provide extra stiffness and strength.

The size of gutters should be determined by the size and spacing of the downspouts used. One square inch (6.45 square cm) of downspout is required for each 100 square feet (9.2 square meters) of roof. If downspouts permit water to flow to the ground instead of to an underground connection to a drain, splash-blocks should be provided to prevent soil erosion under the downspout.

Good ventilation should not be overlooked as the garage area is subject to accumulation of gasoline

Cementing down both the flashing (top) and the cut valley shingles, insures a tight valley that will drain well without leaking.

(Courtesy of Asphalt Roofing Manufacturers Assn.)

Garages should be adequately ventilated and have rain-carrying systems to keep water from damaging the roof and wall construction. Gable end vents are used for both the garage and adjoining storage building of this home. The downspouts each have splash blocks to deposit water away from the foundation. (Photo courtesy of Stephenson Cupolas)

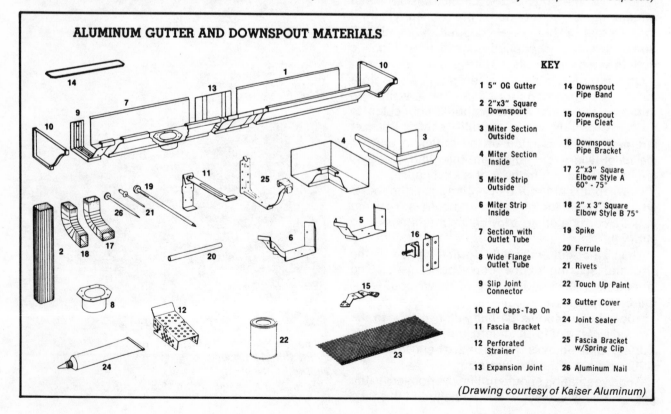

ALUMINUM GUTTER AND DOWNSPOUT MATERIALS

KEY

1 5" OG Gutter

2 2"x3" Square Downspout

3 Miter Section Outside

4 Miter Section Inside

5 Miter Strip Outside

6 Miter Strip Inside

7 Section with Outlet Tube

8 Wide Flange Outlet Tube

9 Slip Joint Connector

10 End Caps-Tap On

11 Fascia Bracket

12 Perforated Strainer

13 Expansion Joint

14 Downspout Pipe Band

15 Downspout Pipe Cleat

16 Downspout Pipe Bracket

17 2"x3" Square Elbow Style A 60° - 75°

18 2" x 3" Square Elbow Style B 75°

19 Spike

20 Ferrule

21 Rivets

22 Touch Up Paint

23 Gutter Cover

24 Joint Sealer

25 Fascia Bracket w/Spring Clip

26 Aluminum Nail

(Drawing courtesy of Kaiser Aluminum)

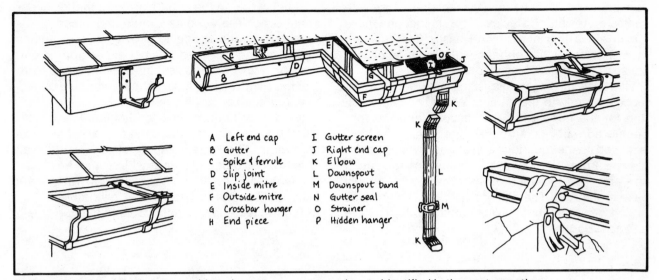

Packaged roof drainage system, with various components and parts identified in the center portion of this sketch, is offered by several aluminum fabricating companies including the Billy Penn Company and Crown Aluminum Company, from whose brochures these items were sketched. Alternative methods of mounting gutters on roof fascia are shown in the side sketches. At left top, a hanger support that fastens directly to the fascia and has a lock-bar (below) which holds the gutter firmly. At top right, a gutter hanger with extension strap that nails to roof sheathing under the shingles. Bottom right, long spike and ferrule method of fastening to fascia. (Drawing by Carol Reschke)

fumes, carbon monoxide, and other chemical vapors. The front of the garage door can be provided with louvers and ceiling vents can be installed to take care of this hazardous condition. Where paints and chemicals are stored in closed cabinets, the door fronts should be louvered.

THE CUPOLA

A cupola is an easily attached item that adds to the decorative style of the garage and is especially compatible with Colonial or Early American architecture. The unit also provides ventilation to the top of the garage.

For instance, Stephenson cupolas are offered in three styles: standard, for contemporary or ranch homes with some colonial features with roof pitches three to six-inch rise per foot (75/300 to 150/300); and the President and Governor series for homes of traditional design with roofs steeper than six-inch rise per foot (150/300).

The position of the cupola on the roof is according to individual taste. If the decision is difficult to make, the roof pitch can be cut into the cupola base and the cupola moved from place to place on the roof and checked for effect before the final installation is completed.

The cupola roof is constructed with exterior plywood which is hand-covered with copper or alumi-

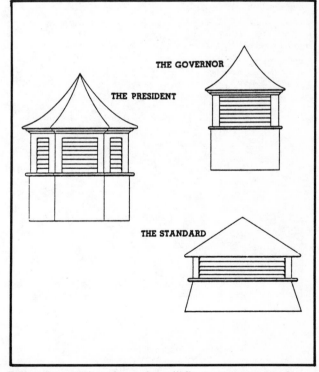

These three styles of cupolas will fit most garage roofs. The units provide ventilation as well as decorative effect. (Drawing courtesy of Stephenson Cupolas)

num sheeting. The sheeting is stapled in place with corrosion-resistant staples. Tower sections have louver sides that allow air to easily flow through them but resist the entrance of precipitation because of the angle of the blades.

The base of the cupola is the only part that attaches directly to the garage. When the final position for the cupola is decided upon and the roof pitch is correctly cut into the cupola base, the base is placed on the roof ridge and aligned with the shingle line. Four 10d box nails or screws of equivalent size are used to attach each corner of the cupola base to the roof. The nail or screw holes should be drilled with a slightly smaller diameter drill bit before nailing is begun.

Finish work on the cupola also is a matter of personal taste. The cupolas should be primed on the outside and the inside to provide a seal against moisture and to guard against expansion or contraction. Many owners seal the outside of the tower and base with a clear finish. Others want the outside to match the color of the house.

The top of the cupola often is completed with a weathervane. Some weathervanes are hand-cast aluminum. There are a variety of ornaments available to sit on different stands with several finishes. A few include an American Eagle, stallion, rooster and sailboat. The stand has special reversible hinged mounting feet that are adjustable to fit each type of cupola.

8
Carports

The popularity of residential carports increases each year as more and more homeowners convert attached garages to added living space, thereby leaving the auto homeless. In many areas of the country, the easily erected carport can provide all the necessary protection needed, keeping the car or cars out of the rain, sun, frost and snow.

Modern carports can be attached to the home or constructed as totally free-standing units adjacent to the dwelling. Such units almost always have a solid roof, may incorporate one or more walls of the house, may have storage units at one end and along the walls, or may simply be a roof supported by four columns with all four sides totally open.

In planning a carport you will need to check the local building code as well as property deed restrictions. Set-back and sideline dimensions are most certain to come into consideration if the new carport is replacing an existing garage or joined to the garage to provide added protection for more than the original number of autos housed on the property.

Unlike more expensive garage construction detailed throughout this book, carport doesn't require doors, windows, foundation walls, full

Drive-through convenience is a feature of this mountain-area carport constructed of redwood to keep with the overall house design. Compacted gravel is used for the driveway, while the carport has an exposed aggregate concrete floor. (Photo courtesy of California Redwood Association)

concrete floor and house-type framing. Economical post-and-beam construction methods, post footings and loose aggregate or narrow concrete drive strips often are sufficient.

Posts for most carports are set in the ground or securely connected to a firm foundation, such as the original concrete driveway, if the carport is simply attached to the front of the original garage. The posts support horizontal beams (plates) which in turn support the roof rafters at right angles to the beams.

For most carports, 4x4 (89x89 mm) and 4x6 (89x140 mm) posts are sufficiently large in size. On larger structures, bigger posts are sometimes nec-

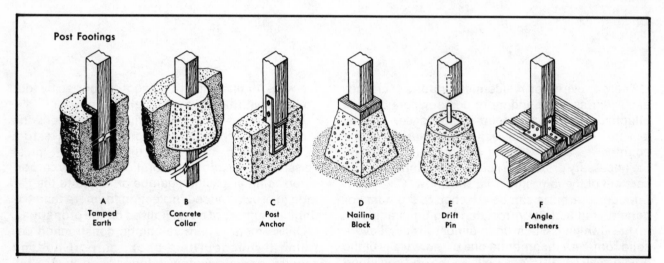

Post footings for carport roof support can be constructed in several ways, always making certain the posts are carefully plumbed with a level. Depth varies according to frost conditions. Usually 36 inches (914.4 mm) is adequate. (Drawings courtesy of California Redwood Association)

Noted designer Barry Berkus used a shed-style carport for this modern home. The carport roof follows the cathedral ceiling of the living room and calls for a finish roofing surface of wood shakes. (Photo courtesy of Barry Berkus)

Center support posts are not required with this aluminum 20x20 foot (6x6 meter) double carport. The unit can be used free-standing or attached to a building. Either six or eight-inch (152.4 or 203.2 mm) I-beams can be specified for 20 or 40 pound (9 or 18 kilograms) loads. (Photo courtesy of Alcan Building Products)

essary to support heavier roof loads and still maintain wide post spacing. Two by four's (38x89 mm) or 2x6's (38x140 mm) are sometimes used in tandem, with spacer blocks between them at 24-inch (609.6 mm) intervals, to form a column instead of a solid post.

Some carport shelters are attached to the existing buildings with a 2x4 (38x89 mm) or larger ledger strip bolted horizontally to the original wall. Such construction permits the building to perform the function of the posts. The rafters rest directly on, and are anchored to, the ledger strip.

Construction heart redwood or pressure-treated posts should be used to prevent decay and all metal parts used in connection with the redwood should be corrosion resistant to avoid iron staining.

The three most commonly used methods of post footings are:

1. Use of a post anchor which is embedded in poured concrete or fastened to existing concrete with a power-actuated stud driver. These type fasteners are commonly available at building material outlets and provide positive anchoring of posts to concrete.
2. A prefabricated concrete-wood nailing block pier can be used to toenail the post to a redwood block set in the precast concrete. The nailing block usually is less secure than the metal anchor bolted through the post.
3. When a concealed anchor is desired, a drift pin often is used. It is embedded in concrete and

CARPORT STORAGE

By adding spacious cabinets to your carport, you can add space to the rest of your house. The large closets shown are four feet deep and eight feet high—large enough to store screens, sports equipment, step ladders, or garbage cans. The smaller cabinets are for almost any kind of tools, tires, out of season clothes, or other odds and ends.

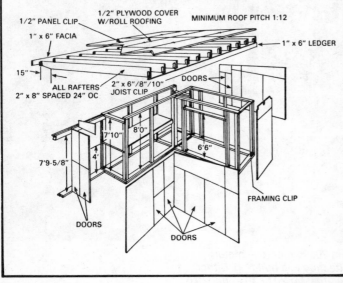

Extending the carport roof beyond the dimension required to adequately protect the automobile can provide a convenient storage area for lawn and garden tools and supplies. This structure has end-opening compartments as well as storage cubicles opening toward the carport area. (Photo courtesy of the American Plywood Association)

(Courtesy of the Panel Clip Company booklet "Build it with Clips")

Post and beam construction is used for this carport and patio shelter. The free-standing unit incorporates a 2-foot 10-inch x 12-foot (.6 meters, 254 mm x 3.6 meters) storage section flanked by a 12-foot (3.6 meters) wide carport on one side and 8-foot (2.4 meters) wide patio on the other. (Drawing courtesy of the American Plywood Association)

A decorative redwood overhang frames the roofless "carport" area of this hillside setting. The brick-paved entry/courtyard is shielded from view by a rustic fence which also provides wind protection in the carport area. (Photo courtesy of California Redwood Association)

61

slips into a same-size hole drilled in the end of the post/column. The California Redwood Association suggests that if this method is used, a small space should be left between the bottom of the post and the concrete surface to avoid the accumulation of moisture and dirt. A washer is good for this purpose.

Basic roof designs used in carport construction include a flat roof, a sloping or shed roof attached to another structure, a gable roof and a pyramid roof. The flat and shed roof are by far the most commonly employed in carport design. The gable and pyramid roofs are somewhat more complicated for the home handyman, but they are basic roof designs and offer the possibility of additional overhead storage space.

Appearance is often the deciding factor in the design of the roof as the new structure should be compatible with the basic house design and not something that appears to have been mistakenly dropped in place on a lost weekend. No matter what type the roof, it should be slightly sloped to allow moisture run-off and should be at least eight feet (2.4 meters) high to allow for head clearance in all

For the homeowner who only wants to protect his car from the weather, here is the ideal carport. (Photo courtesy of Alcan Building Products)

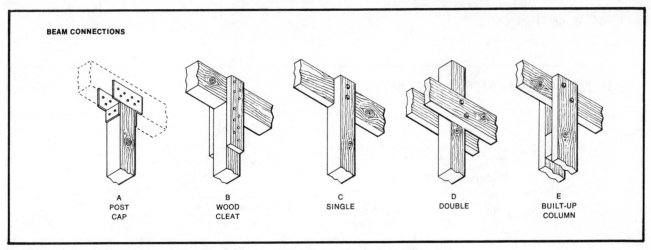

BEAM CONNECTIONS

A
POST
CAP

B
WOOD
CLEAT

C
SINGLE

D
DOUBLE

E
BUILT-UP
COLUMN

Carport roof beams can be attached to support posts in various ways as indicated here. A metal post cap is the quickest and easiest to use when the beam is the same width as the post. (Drawings courtesy of California Redwood Association)

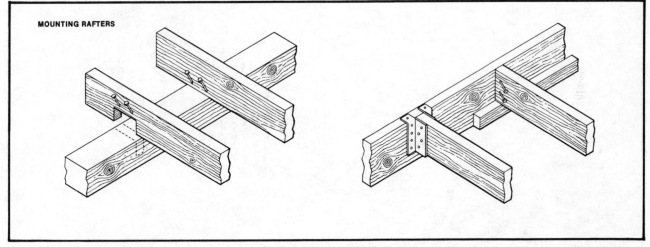

MOUNTING RAFTERS

Carport roof rafters can be mounted on beams by (left to right) notching, toenailing, metal hangers, or toenailing above a ledger strip. When rafters extend from an existing building, they may be attached either flush or on top of a ledger strip fastened to the building. (Drawings courtesy of California Redwood Association)

areas. The height of the carport should not interfere with surrounding objects such as utility poles or wires.

The beams which support roof rafters also tie the posts together and give rigidity to the structure. To perform these functions properly, adequate beam sizes must be used and the beams must be adequately connected to the posts. Building materials dealers can provide you with durable beam connections that are easy to use and provide maximum strength.

Prefabricated trusses are generally used for gabled and hipped roofs whose slopes fall in the range between 3-in-12 and 6-in-12 (75/300 and 150/300) pitches (3 or 6 inch rise for every foot of horizontal run or distance). With flat roofs, the rafters support the finished roof and their loading strength must be calculated to support both the ceiling and roof loads (snow). In application, flat-roof joist-rafters are set

and assembled like floor joists. Greater strength and faster assembly can be accomplished with metal rafter hangers.

Flat roofs can be sheathed with plywood which serves as a decking material for gravel surfacing applied with hot asphalt or pitch. Sloping roofs also may have a plywood or lumber deck to which composition shingle or wood shingles or shakes may be applied.

Aside from post-and-beam construction, many residential carports are constructed with side or end walls (or both) matching existing house walls. This is especially popular where the carport will function as a drive-through involving a circular driveway.

Carports constructed by conventional or post-and-beam methods provide an excellent opportunity to include a secured good-size storage area for bikes, lawn equipment and the like. Exterior grade plywood can be combined with siding, brick or

BUILD AN ATTACHED CARPORT

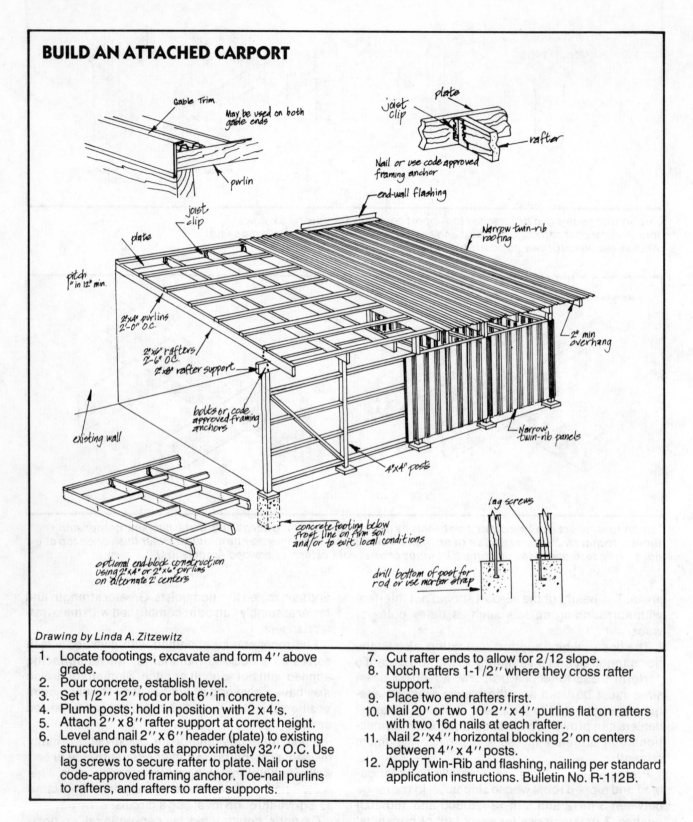

Drawing by Linda A. Zitzewitz

1. Locate foootings, excavate and form 4'' above grade.
2. Pour concrete, establish level.
3. Set 1/2'' 12'' rod or bolt 6'' in concrete.
4. Plumb posts; hold in position with 2 x 4's.
5. Attach 2'' x 8'' rafter support at correct height.
6. Level and nail 2'' x 6'' header (plate) to existing structure on studs at approximately 32'' O.C. Use lag screws to secure rafter to plate. Nail or use code-approved framing anchor. Toe-nail purlins to rafters, and rafters to rafter supports.

7. Cut rafter ends to allow for 2/12 slope.
8. Notch rafters 1-1/2'' where they cross rafter support.
9. Place two end rafters first.
10. Nail 20' or two 10' 2'' x 4'' purlins flat on rafters with two 16d nails at each rafter.
11. Nail 2''x4'' horizontal blocking 2' on centers between 4'' x 4'' posts.
12. Apply Twin-Rib and flashing, nailing per standard application instructions. Bulletin No. R-112B.

Twenty-four-inch (609.6 mm) wide Twin-Rib aluminum panels, available in eight, 10 and 12-foot (2.4, 3 and 3.6 meters) lengths, are used for the roof and partial walls of this attached carport. Panels can be cut with a hacksaw and also can be end-lapped to provide necessary extended length. (Plan and instructions courtesy of Kaiser)

block in keeping with the house exterior design. A minimum depth of four feet (1.2 meters) is recommended for such storage areas, whether located on the sides or at the rear of the structure.

Location and design of storage walls of the carport should take into consideration the effect they will have on blocking daylight and summer breezes from the house. Such storage areas also can be beneficial in sheltering the house from winter winds. A desirable southern exposure should not be blocked by a carport wall.

Two additional approaches to carport construction are packaged aluminum assemblies and fiberglass panel-wood or ornamental iron framework systems highly familiar in patio cover construction. Such systems are sold with all necessary materials and fasteners, and include step-by-step instructions for assembly.

9
Garage Doors

Buying a garage door is very much like shopping for a new suit of clothes in a large department store — you are going to see literally hundreds of styles, models, types and sizes. But a big difference is that you'll be looking at the units on catalog pages and won't have the benefit of holding them up in the sunlight to see exactly how they will appear in use.

Today's garage doors are great improvements over the old barn-style doors that were heavy, swinging and strap-hinged to the opening. Those who grew up with these doors well remember their blowing off in a storm, their sticking closed with every ground swell and their inability to open until all the snow was removed from in front of the garage. Many families resorted to keeping the snow shovel in the house — for it was impossible to get it from the garage if you couldn't get the doors open!

The biggest change in all this took place in the early 1920's with the invention of the upward-acting "overhead" garage door, a sectional unit that today is common to almost every new housing development. Since that time many refinements have been made in design and one-piece flush-type overhead styles have been added.

SELECTION

In choosing a garage door, realize that no other single item on your home is larger. Up to 30 percent of what a visitor may see when approaching your home is the garage door. It is essential that the door be in keeping with the architectural style of your home.

Size is the first consideration in the choice of the garage door, in relation to both width and height. The garage door industry in describing a door size always quotes the width of the opening first followed by the height of the opening. The garage door goes inside the building and is sealed on two sides and the top with stop molding; therefore, the door and the opening have the exact same size. The final size of the opening after the installation of the door is reduced by the thickness of the stop molding.

Over the years the most popular height has traditionally been seven feet (2.1 meters). However, in recent years 7-feet 6-inches (2.1 meters, 152.4 mm) and 8-foot (2.4 meters) heights have become widely used to accommodate recreational vehicles and boats. Other models available include 6-feet 6-inches (1.8 meters, 152.4 mm) and custom heights manufactured to special order.

During the age of the larger car, (it's going the opposite direction now), the popular garage door width increased from seven or eight feet (2.1 or 2.4 meters) to nine feet (2.7 meters) for a single-car opening. Still other one-car doors are offered in 10 and 12-foot (3 and 3.6 meters) widths.

For multiple-car garages, you can use two or more single-car doors with a dividing column in between, or choose standard 16 or 18-foot (4.8 or 5.4 meters) wide doors or custom sizes. Automatic door operators (detailed on later pages) are designed to close and open all standard sizes.

Overhead doors are manufactured in both single-piece flush style and multi-panel sectional style. The latter type is usually four or five equal-size sections assembled on-site according to specific instructions included with a complete hardware package.

Both one-piece flush and sectional garage doors are offered in a choice of construction materials. They include:

- **Wood-Plywood-Hardboard:** These units may be a combination of materials with facing skins laminated to a selection of core stocks, including energy-saving foam, or may be solid wood with individual panels of solid stock.

GARAGE DOOR DESIGNS

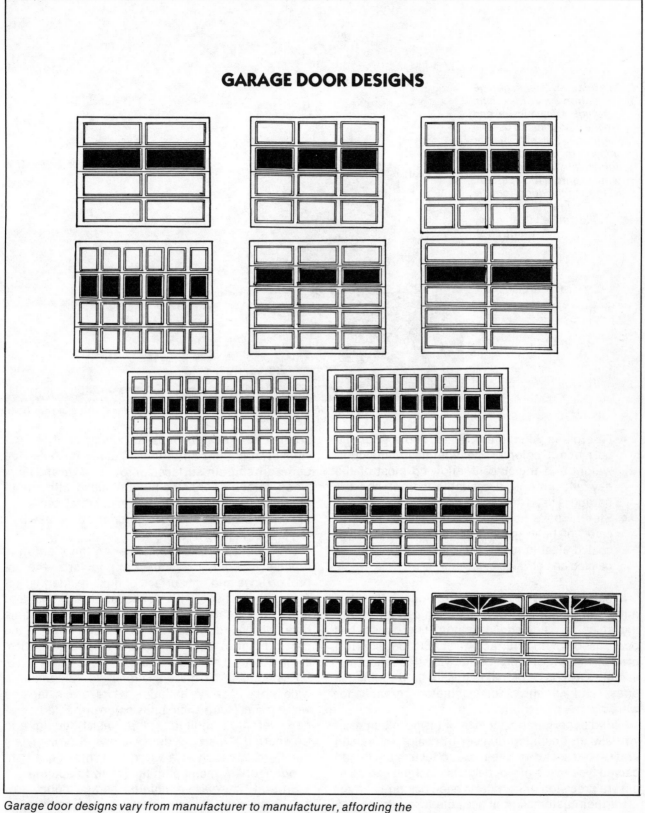

Garage door designs vary from manufacturer to manufacturer, affording the homeowner a choice of solid door or various glazed panels positioned at eye level or above. These typical designs are made of kiln-dried lumber for use on a 12 or 15-inch (304.8 or 381 mm) radial track. (Drawings courtesy of Clopay's Overhead Door Products Division)

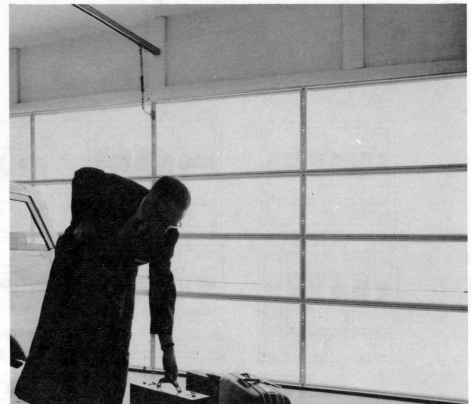

Fiberglass overhang garage doors give maximum daylight transmission and make it possible to use the garage as a cold-weather playroom for children. This lightweight unit is equipped with an automatic operator. Lighting the door from the inside at night helps to illuminate the driveway entrance.

Reprinted, by permission, Schram, *Improving the Outside of Your Home*

- **Fiberglass Aluminum:** These doors offer the permanent color of the fiberglass, are lightweight and translucent, allowing most of the daylight through, a desirable factor when the garage is used as a workshop.
- **Steel:** These easy-to-operate doors are fabricated of heavy-gauge, electro-galvanized zinc-coated steel to resist rust and are factory-prime painted on both sides.

In selecting a wood garage door, check to determine that kiln-dried wood has been used for framing, stiles, rails and edge finishing. If hardboard has been used for the surface, it should be exterior-grade. Finger-jointing of individual section assemblies also is desirable as this method eliminates stress and minimizes or eliminates potential for warping.

Wood panel garage doors offer the possibilities of virtually an unlimited number of designs in raised and carved sections. The most popular is the raised carved type made of wood that is machine carved to assure precision uniformity in each design.

Further customizing is possible through the use of a variety of applied moldings. Frequently, the paneled doors incorporate one horizontal section of glass windows which also may be embellished with architectural design trims to complement the design of adjoining structures. Totally flush facade doors are smooth-surfaced or rough-sawn and most wood garage doors may be purchased with an optional wood preservative treatment that seals out moisture, protects against fungus and assures a better, longer lasting door.

The widespread acceptance of the California ranch-style home has helped to popularize the unbroken lines and flat surface of flush residential garage doors. These units don't trap dirt or dust and thus are virtually maintenance free. At the same time, this type door can be customized through the use of paint or applied designs of wood, plastics, stamped metal or hardboard.

Residential fiberglass sectional doors come in a wide range of colors including white, green, tan and wood grains, with some units color-protected by ultra-violet light inhibitors that resist fading and weathering. This type door weighs approximately one-third as much as a wood door making it light enough for any member of the family to operate.

Several fiberglass-aluminum garage doors now on the market are assembled with hinges or joints which totally eliminate the possibility of pinching your fingers between sections when closing the door. These designs also assure a weathertight

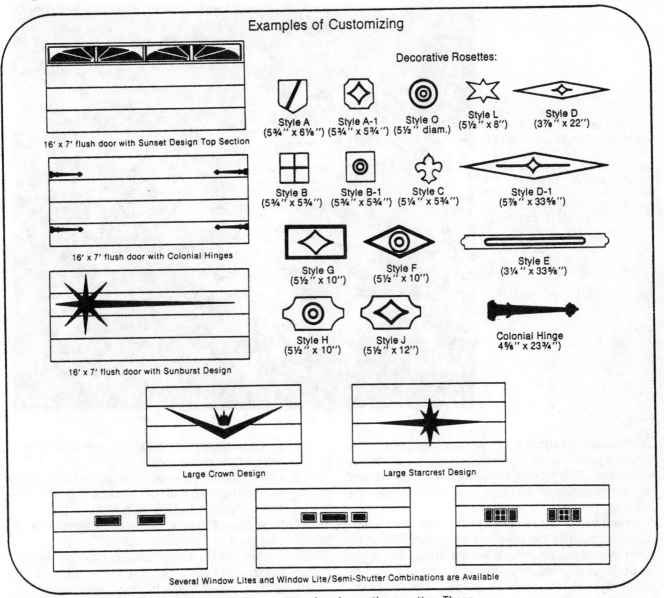

Examples of Customizing

16' x 7' flush door with Sunset Design Top Section

16' x 7' flush door with Colonial Hinges

16' x 7' flush door with Sunburst Design

Decorative Rosettes:

Style A
(5¾'' x 6⅛'')

Style A-1
(5¾'' x 5¾'')

Style O
(5½'' diam.)

Style L
(5½'' x 8'')

Style D
(3⅞'' x 22'')

Style B
(5¾'' x 5¾'')

Style B-1
(5¾'' x 5¾'')

Style C
(5¼'' x 5¾'')

Style D-1
(5⅞'' x 33⅝'')

Style G
(5½'' x 10'')

Style F
(5½'' x 10'')

Style E
(3¼'' x 33⅝'')

Style H
(5½'' x 10'')

Style J
(5½'' x 12'')

Colonial Hinge
4⅝'' x 23¾'')

Large Crown Design

Large Starcrest Design

Several Window Lites and Window Lite/Semi-Shutter Combinations are Available

Wood garage doors can be customized in many ways using decorative rosettes. These items indicate a few of the possible treatments for both flush doors and those with windows. (Drawing courtesy of Clopay)

joint. Maintenance of fiberglass doors is accomplished with an occasional wash down with a garden hose. Repainting is unnecessary.

Sectional and one-piece steel garage doors are now manufactured to give the appearance of wood rather than the old corrugated industrial-look long associated with this type door. Steel units are offered in horizontal panel and embossed raised panel designs, with or without windows and shutters.

An important benefit of one steel garage door is exceptionally low headroom clearance of just 1-3/4 inches (44.45 mm) compared to the usual 10-1/2 inches (266.7 mm).

Space requirements should be given careful attention in purchasing a new garage door. Sideroom, headroom, backroom and center post requirements vary according to door sizes and hardware selected. For example, one sectional door operating on a 15-inch (381 mm) track radius requires 10-3/4 inches (273 mm) headroom, 3-3/4 inches (95.2 mm) sideroom, backroom of door height plus 12 inches (304.8 mm) and a minimum 8-inch (203.2 mm) center post. An optional 12-inch (304.8 mm) radius track for the same door will reduce the headroom needed to 8-3/4 inches (222.2 mm). It should also be noted that most doors on the market can be purchased with

Raised panel garage doors designs are available in steel as well as wood. This door is a raised panel sectional offered in eight, nine, 16 and 18-foot (2.4, 2.7, 4.8 and 5.4 meters) widths and 7-foot (2.1 meters) height. Joint design virtually eliminates pinched fingers. (Photo courtesy of Stanley)

optional low headroom kits which reduce the headroom required to approximately five inches (127 mm). This type of installation may be required to permit garage storage of a truck or recreational vehicle.

Assembly of a new door in the finished garage opening is within the talents of many handy persons, but it would be advisable to seek professional help if in doubt of your ability to undertake the project. You also may wish to specifically ask your building materials dealer if the door you are considering has been designed for homeowner assembly and installation. If it has, it will be sold with easy-to-read and understandable instructions in step-by-step fashion.

One such door on the market is made by Frantz Manufacturing Co., which condenses the operation to these 12 steps:

1. Unpack all the hardware. (Warranty requires painting of wood doors before installation.) Fasten bolts in first door section to hinges and hangers.
2. Fasten hinge hanger to each end of the door section.
3. Attach the U-bar brace (not required with all doors).
4. Insert rollers into hangers.
5. Place bottom door section in the door opening and check for level.
6. Place Number Two section on first door section and attach with hinges and hangers. Do this with each door section.
7. Now place tracks over the vertical rollers and bolt track to the door jamb.
8. Fasten the vertical track, curved track and horizontal track to jamb angle at top of door and the entire assembly is installed.
9. Temporarily secure the horizontal track to ceiling joist with rope.
10. Install top hangers in upper corners of top door section.
11. Raise all sections of door into horizontal track and secure in place. Attach the springs and cables.
12. Make final adjustments: set spring tension, tighten nuts and bolts, etc.

While these instructions are brief, full details are provided with each door and help to provide answers to such basic problems as how to level the first panel so all others will be level when set in place.

If the garage door you purchase doesn't come complete with perimeter insulation, you may wish to

*Horizontal panel sectional garage doors complement most any architectural style.
This steel unit is available in widths 8 to 18 feet (2.4 to 5.4 meters) and heights 6-feet
6-inches to 8-feet (1.8 meters, 152.4 mm to 2.4 meters). The steel doors are prime
painted at the factory and can be insulated with lightweight fiberglass panels that
slide into the interior framework. (Photo courtesy of Stanley)*

71

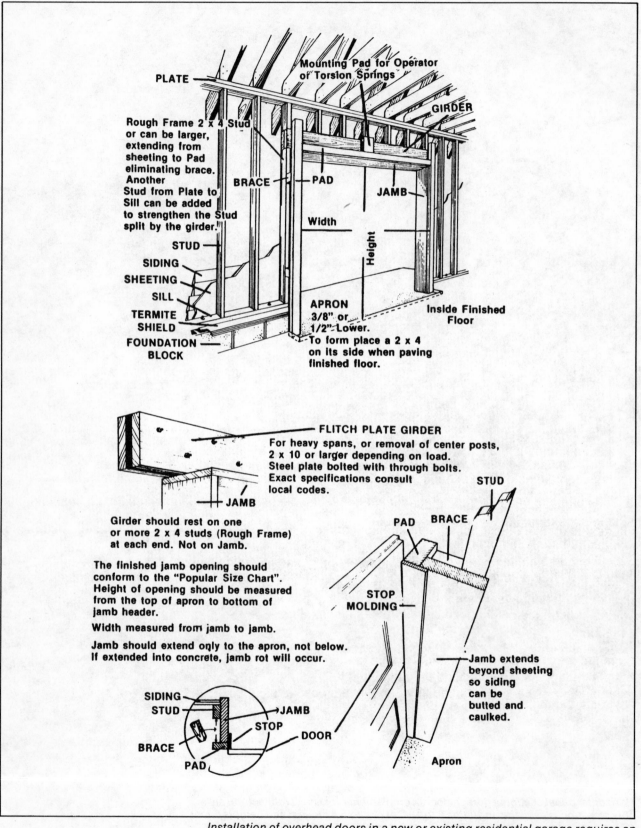

PLATE

Mounting Pad for Operator of Torsion Springs

GIRDER

Rough Frame 2 x 4 Stud or can be larger, extending from sheeting to Pad eliminating brace. Another Stud from Plate to Sill can be added to strengthen the Stud split by the girder."

BRACE — PAD

JAMB

Width

Height

STUD

SIDING

SHEETING

SILL

TERMITE SHIELD

FOUNDATION BLOCK

APRON 3/8" or 1/2" Lower. To form place a 2 x 4 on its side when paving finished floor.

Inside Finished Floor

FLITCH PLATE GIRDER

For heavy spans, or removal of center posts, 2 x 10 or larger depending on load. Steel plate bolted with through bolts. Exact specifications consult local codes.

JAMB

Girder should rest on one or more 2 x 4 studs (Rough Frame) at each end. Not on Jamb.

The finished jamb opening should conform to the "Popular Size Chart". Height of opening should be measured from the top of apron to bottom of jamb header.

Width measured from jamb to jamb.

Jamb should extend only to the apron, not below. If extended into concrete, jamb rot will occur.

STUD

PAD   BRACE

STOP MOLDING

Jamb extends beyond sheeting so siding can be butted and caulked.

Apron

SIDING

STUD

JAMB

STOP

BRACE

DOOR

PAD

Installation of overhead doors in a new or existing residential garage requires an opening that is square, plumb and the same size as the door. These drawings show various framing details accepted by local building codes. (Drawings courtesy of Ridge Doors)

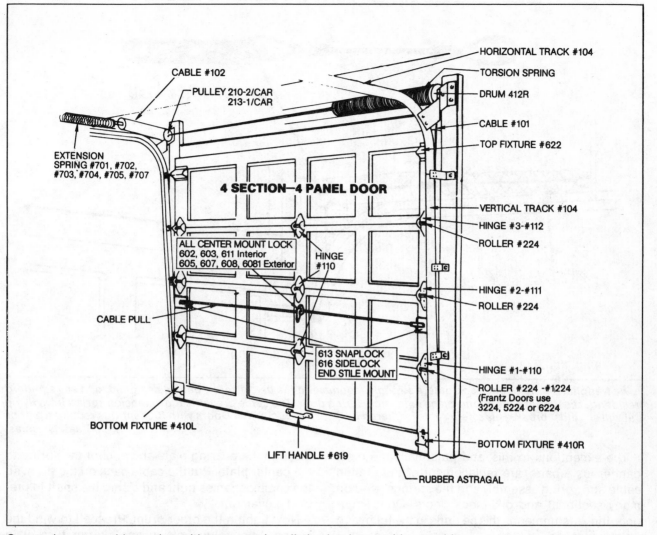

CABLE #102

PULLEY 210-2/CAR 213-1/CAR

HORIZONTAL TRACK #104

TORSION SPRING

DRUM 412R

CABLE #101

TOP FIXTURE #622

EXTENSION SPRING #701, #702, #703, #704, #705, #707

4 SECTION—4 PANEL DOOR

VERTICAL TRACK #104

HINGE #3-#112

ROLLER #224

ALL CENTER MOUNT LOCK
602, 603, 611 Interior
605, 607, 608, 6081 Exterior

HINGE #110

HINGE #2-#111

ROLLER #224

CABLE PULL

613 SNAPLOCK
616 SIDELOCK
END STILE MOUNT

HINGE #1-#110

ROLLER #224 -#1224
(Frantz Doors use
3224, 5224 or 6224)

BOTTOM FIXTURE #410L

LIFT HANDLE #619

BOTTOM FIXTURE #410R

RUBBER ASTRAGAL

Garage doors are sold complete with necessary installation hardware, with assembly taking place at the site. This drawing indicates typical hardware identified by company ordering number. The firm specializes in supplying parts for homeowner door repair and ships each item with complete installation instructions. (Drawing courtesy of Door Products, Inc.)

purchase one of the do-it-yourself kits available from building material dealers. Of various designs, these insulations are easy to cut to needed lengths and apply to door or frame to seal out wind, rain, snow and cold while helping to conserve energy. Usually only a saw, hammer, knife, tacks and glue are required to complete the installation.

GARAGE DOOR MAINTENANCE

Occasional lubrication of moving hardware parts of sectional and single-panel overhead doors usually will keep the units in fine operating order. However, accidental damage or worn parts may require replacement and repair from time to time.

Most of the hardware parts used by manufacturers in assembling their respective brand-name models are standard and thus interchangeable on other doors. Local building material dealers frequently have a "repair headquarters" display of such parts. Should they not have one in your area, you can obtain them by mail from Door Products, Inc., Bensenville, Illinois, or Ridge Doors of Monmouth Junction, New Jersey. The latter firm has a nationwide toll free number — 1-(800) 631-5656 — for your convenience.

Most garage door replacement parts can be quickly and easily put in place with a wrench or screwdriver and require no more instruction than to remember carefully how the old part came off the door or jamb.

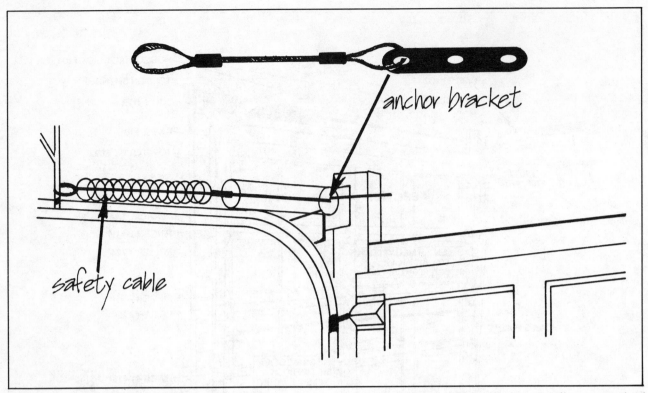

The National Safety Council and others strongly recommend the use of safety cables designed to fit any standard residential sectional style or one-piece extension spring door. The cable prevents the extension spring from flying at will should it break. This safety cable is offered by Door Products, Inc. Doors with four springs require a pair of safety cables.

The exceptions to this, and potentially the most dangerous repairs, are replacement of the torsion cable and spring assembly and the springs used on many sectional and one-piece doors. Door Products, Inc., recommends this be done in the following careful manner.

Close and lock the door. If the door has two springs, unwind the good spring with a pair of winding rods about 14 inches (355.6 mm) long. Do not use a pipe wrench or screw driver.

To unwind the spring, put one rod into the winding plug hole and hold the rod firmly. Undo the set screws slowly and you will feel the spring push or pull against the rod. When both screws are removed, let the rod rest against the door or header and place the second rod in the next hole. Hold firmly and remove the first rod. Do this until the spring is completely unwound. (Reverse this procedure when you wind the spring. You will push against the pressure.)

Once you have all the tension off the spring, undo both drums and file the set screw burrs. Undo the spring from the center and slide to the end of the shaft. Pull the shaft out of the bearing plate and take the drum off, then the spring. Take off the plugs and replace on the new spring. Put the new spring back on the shaft with the drum. Slide the shaft back through the bearing plate and anchor the spring to the center plate. Put the cable back on the drum so the cable becomes tight and clamp the shaft to prevent movement.

Now tighten the other drum. Proceed to wind the spring. Each plug hole is one-quarter turn on a spring. Put seven full turns on a spring to start. If it's fast or hard to lift, add or remove the required amount of one-quarter turns needed to obtain proper balance. Oil the spring and bearings when good balance is obtained, but do not use grease.

For replacement of pulley, roller, extension springs, extension cables and bottom fixture the garage door should be in the open position and secured there with a 2x4 (38x89 mm) prop or step ladder under the door.

With the springs in a relaxed position and no tension on the cable, pull the cable at the anchor point and disconnect. Remove and replace the spring, cable, pulley, bottom fixture or bottom roller. Be sure to note how the cable goes over the stationary pulley through the spring pulley and back to the anchor point.

Securely fasten the cable and tighten all bolts. The length of the cable under tension should be equal on both sides of the door for proper balance. If the door is not balanced, repeat the above and increase or decrease the tension by changing the length of the cable.

Among the replacement parts available from Door Products, Inc., is a new safety cable that fits any standard residential sectional-style of one-piece extension spring door. The low-cost item is highly recommended for use in both new installations and while replacing a broken assembly. It prevents the spring assembly from flying at will when breaking, causing serious damage or injury.

This safety cable is pulled through the center of the spring with one end bolted to the back hang of the door track and the other end to the door frame. When the spring gives out, it is held in place by the cable rather than possibly shooting wildly into the garage.

The chart below can help you determine the correct replacement extension spring when one breaks. It also is recommended that you take the broken spring with you to your building materials outlet when purchasing a replacement unit.

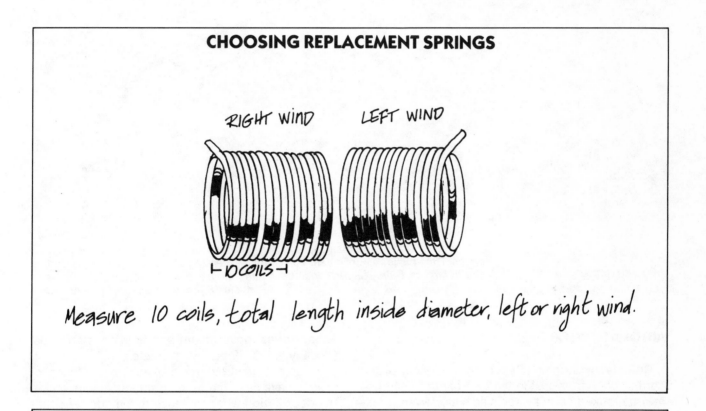

CHOOSING REPLACEMENT SPRINGS

RIGHT WIND   LEFT WIND

⊢ 10 COILS ⊣

Measure 10 coils, total length inside diameter, left or right wind.

	DOOR SIZE	EXTENSION SPRING
110 lb. Blue	8 ft. wide x 6 ft. 6 in. high	2 panel — 4 sections
120 lb. Green	8 ft. wide x 7 ft. high	2 panel — 4 sections
130 lb. Black	8 ft. wide x 7 ft. high	4 panel — 4 sections
140 lb. Red	9 ft. wide x 7 ft. high	2 panel — 4 sections
150 lb. White	9 ft. wide x 7 ft. high	4 panel — 4 sections
150 lb. White	16 ft. wide x 7 ft. high	4 panel — 4 sections (4 springs)
150 lb. Silver	9 ft. wide x 7 ft. high	4 panel — 4 sections (4 springs)
150 lb. Silver	16 ft. wide x 7 ft. high	4 panel — 4 sections (4 springs)

FOR OTHER SPRING SIZES, MEASURE 10 COILS, LENGTH WITHOUT ENDS, INSIDE DIAMETER, HOW WIDE IS THE DOOR? HOW HIGH? PANELS IN EACH SECTION AND HOW MANY SECTIONS.

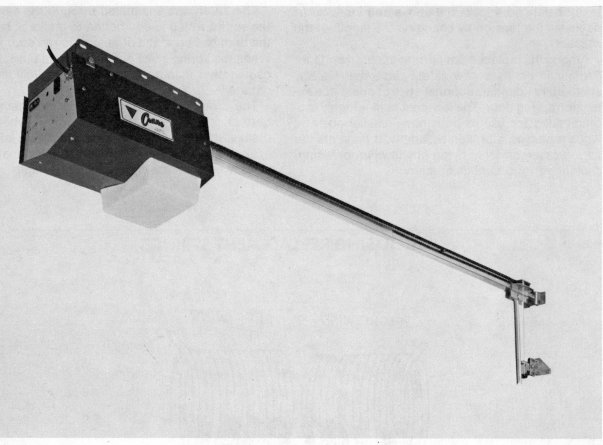

Another kind of automatic garage door operator has a 1/3-HP motor and is chain driven. The unit has a convenient pull chain to operate garage lights when the door is not in use. Safety features include instant reverse in close cycle and stop in open cycle. (Photo courtesy of H.W. Crane Co.)

AUTOMATIC DOOR OPENERS

Completely automatic opening or closing of the garage door from inside the car, garage or house may be looked upon by some as a modern-day luxury, but to those who use an automatic door operator the unit affords comfort, convenience and safety.

Easy to install, these automatic door operators go into action at the push of a button with most units controlling the garage light simultaneously. Units automatically open, close, lock and unlock the garage door, turn on the light and then turn it off in a couple of minutes.

Automatic garage door operators are manufactured by more than a dozen firms and are sold as a package with all the materials required for complete installation. Units vary a bit in shape and design and most manufacturers offer various horsepower (HP) sizes keyed to the type and weight door to be operated. These HP ratings range from 1/4 to 1/3, 1/2, 3/4, 1 and up and are designed to meet Underwriters'

Laboratories, government and industry standards. (Usually, a 1/3-HP size is adequate.)

These design standards also assure you that provisions have been made for automatically reversing the door action when, in closing, the door encounters an obstruction. Thus, should a ladder, bike or other object be in the way, the door automatically reverses to the full open position.

Some models on the market also feature an "opening obstruction stop" which prevents the door from opening if it is obstructed during the opening cycle. This feature prevents possible door damage. Still another operational feature of some units is a "command stop" which permits you to partially open or close the door for special conditions, such as permitting a pet to enter or leave the garage.

Automatic garage door operators are equipped with a manual release in case of power failure or other emergency. By simply pulling a lever you may then operate the door manually until power resumes and you push the lever the opposite direction.

A computer-command screw-drive door operator has a one-piece aluminum housing to provide support the full length of the screw-drive. The unit plugs into a standard electrical outlet, has a solid-state micro-computer control at the back of the housing, convenience light at the front and can be easily disengaged for manual operation by simply pulling a rope cord. (Photo courtesy of NuTone)

One-piece garage doors (as well as sectionals) can be equipped with automatic operators by attaching the operator arm to the top-center door rail. Standard side-mounted spring assemblies stabilize the door during movement. (Photo courtesy of H. W. Crane Co.)

The basic design of residential-type automatic door operators employs either a one-piece or multi-section trolley track of steel or aluminum to accomodate the screw-drive or chain-drive mechanism connected to a door-connecting arm. Screw-type units are sometimes more quiet in operation, function more smoothly and are longer lasting. Chain-type units are pre-lubricated in most instances and some are oil infused to eliminate the need for periodic oiling.

As this book was being written, national marketing was initiated for still another type of electronically-controlled automatic garage door opener said to be "the first completely new design in operators in 30 years." Called the Power-Trak™ 600, it's made by Windsor Door, a division of Ceco Corp.

The Power Trak™ 600 features a unique linear drive mechanism. It operates by means of drive links enclosed by a sprocketless drive track engineered to permit links to move only in a pull-push straight line mode to raise and lower the door. The operator is fully controlled by a solid state digital mini-computer programmed to respond either to an in-door switch or to a privately coded transmitter in the car.

The enclosed linear drive has eliminated looping chains, screw drives and exposed chain sprockets, providing low-noise, long-wear operation, according to pre-market testing.

Most automatic garage door openers are designed to accomodate either sectional or one-piece doors of wood, fiberglass or steel up to 18 feet (5.4 meters) wide and seven feet (2.1 meters) high. Special models or adaptor kits are used for doors of greater height.

In purchasing an automatic garage door operator it's best to go shopping with some basic information at your fingertips so you can easily determine the operator model which best meets your specific needs. Among these facts are:

- Type of door (wood, steel, fiberglass) and its dimensions.
- Type of hardware used: tracks for sectional, tracks for one-piece door, or jamb-mounted hardware for one-piece door.
- The headroom clearance above the high point of door travel over the center line of the door. A minimum usually is 1-3/4 inches (44.4 mm), but less space is sometimes required by notching the door or by using a low bracket headroom accessory kit.

- The backroom clearance, usually 10 feet (3 meters) or more from the front of the door opening toward the back wall, is required to accomodate the operator.

All automatic garage door operator makers will strongly caution that their products are not the solution to a damaged or improperly installed garage door. Garage doors must operate smoothly by hand to insure safe and satisfactory performance of an automatic operator. Make certain all hardware is tight. Tighten all loose nuts and screws. Oil rollers and bearings.

Garage doors should be in good balance for best automatic operation. A balanced door will stay in any position of its travel or nearly so. If necessary, have the springs adjusted, but do not remove them! If the strength of the springs has weakened, it is best to contact a qualified garage door mechanic for replacements. Door springs can cause serious injury and should not be adjusted by someone unfamiliar with the dangers involved.

Major marketing of residential automatic garage door operators has brought about the availability of packaged units weighing less than 50 pounds (22.6 kilograms) for convenient store-to-home transportation in an automobile trunk. These units generally have a three-piece trolley track which is bolted together rather than the one-piece track models preferred by most professional installers.

The homeowner models take but several hours to install in new or existing garages with complete

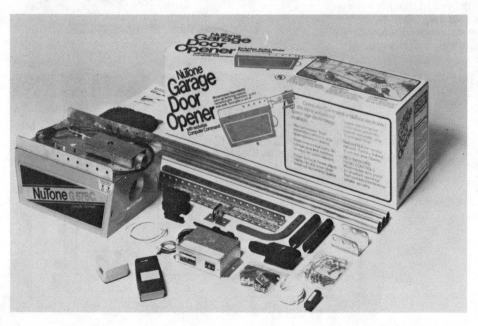

Automatic garage door openers are now packaged and sold by retail building material dealers for homeowner assembly and installation. The unit fits a hatchback or truck and comes complete with all necessary hardware, wire and components, plus a step-by-step installation booklet. (Photo courtesy of Nutone)

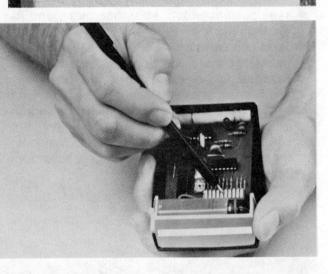

DIGITAL DOOR OPENERS

Among the newest advances in automatic garage door openers is the use of digital radio control which eliminates signal duplication and frequency overlap. This new compact transmitter and receiver permit the homeowner to select his own frequency from 1024 possible settings. If another control or CB radio matches his code, the digital control owner can quickly and easily reset his own frequency by flipping a few miniature switches. (Photo courtesy of Stanley)

Another digital radio control has advanced circuitry which lets the owner choose from a series of on/off positions on the eight-digit switches contained in both transmitter and receiver. Two radio frequencies, 320MHz and 360 MHz, provide 256 digital operating codes each. For two-door garages equipped with separate operators, different frequencies are used. Electronic circuitry in the receiver is protected by a sturdy polystyrene case which has a pre-attached antenna, and a three-wire cable for connection to the operator. The transmitter operates from a self-contained nine-volt battery. (Photo courtesy of Nutone)

step-by-step instructions included with each opener. In its simplest form, such an installation involves six steps:

1. First make sure the door works well manually. Then attach the wall mounting bracket over the door. Attach the housing of tubular rail to the bracket.
2. Hang the power unit from the ceiling or joists.
3. Assemble door arms. Attach upper arm to trolley and lower arm to door mounting bracket.
4. Mount the pushbutton control on the wall near the door to the house.
5. Attach the radio receiver to the power unit terminals on the power unit.
6. Connect the power unit to the power source, a 110-V, 60-cycle outlet.

These basic installation steps are usually broken down fully into movement-by-movement sequence to assure trouble-free installation by the home handyman.

Garage door operators can be permanently wired to the house or simply plugged into a three-prong socket like other household appliances, depending upon local building code requirements. The wall-mounted operational control is connected to the operator power unit with low-voltage wire. Care should be taken to locate wall push buttons out of the reach of very young children who may wish to play "up-and-down-the-door time."

Today's transmitter controls are far superior to those first offered with automatic garage door operators and you can choose digital or standard radio units not much larger than a pack of cigarettes. These units need not be wired to your car as they conveniently clip on the sun visor, are held in a bracket under the dashboard or stored in the glove compartment.

The newest type control is the digital which incorporates advanced integrated circuitry and lets you set your own personal code. NuTone's Model 597, for example, provides a choice of 256 operating codes, virtually eliminating chance duplication with other neighborhood automatic door operators. And if duplication does occur, you simply move the switches to a new position and you have a new code.

Standard radio controls long used in the industry operate in the UHF part of the radio spectrum with a usual choice of a half dozen stock frequencies. These controls give way in preference to digital controls for areas with side-by-side opener installations and in large tract housing projects.

Troubleshooting

From time to time garage door operators may fail to function in the manner intended. Most manufacturers will provide a specific troubleshooting guide for the model which will permit you to solve the

81

problem without calling the service center or a garage door control outlet. Of course, every garage door opener should be checked periodically for lubrication and maintenance conditions.

Here are a few of the basic suggestions which pertain to most models:

TROUBLE	CAUSE	REMEDY
1. Operator fails to run after it has been running excessively.	Excessive running will cause motor to shut off to prevent overheating.	Wait about eight minutes or so, then try again.
2. Operator doesn't run when activated by wall push button or radio transmitter.	No electrical power for operator.	If there is a wall switch, be sure it's on. Using another electrical device, check outlet where operator is plugged in. If operator is wired directly to house wiring, check other devices on same circuit. Check house fuse or circuit breaker.
3. Light doesn't work.	Bulb.	Replace bulb.
4. Reduced operating range of radio control.	Weak battery.	Replace battery.
5. Operator doesn't run when activated by wall pushbutton, but does run when activated by radio transmitter.	Defective pushbutton or wiring problem.	Consult operator manual for specific instructions related to your model.
6. Operator doesn't run when activated by radio transmitter, but does run when activated by wall pushbutton.	Possible defect in transmitter or receiver. Weak battery in radio transmitter. Code in digital transmitter may not match receiver's code.	Replace battery, return controls to supplier, or recode operator.
7. Operator motor starts but doesn't move, moves erratically, reverses, or stops.	Door out of alignment, obstruction to door movement or loose belt drive.	Disengage the trolley from the trolley drive and move the door manually. Correct any binding. If loose belt drive, follow manual for specific tightening instructions.
8. Door doesn't open or close fully.	Door force adjustments too sensitive, door track out of line, broken door roller, door spring out of adjustment, limit finger out of adjustment.	Check each, adjust or replace following instruction manual.
9. Door goes down until it touches floor and then reverses.	Obstruction, ice or snow build-up, or floor upheaval.	Remove obstruction, if necessary. For temporary ice build-up or floor upheaval, reprogram the operator to compensate for such conditions.

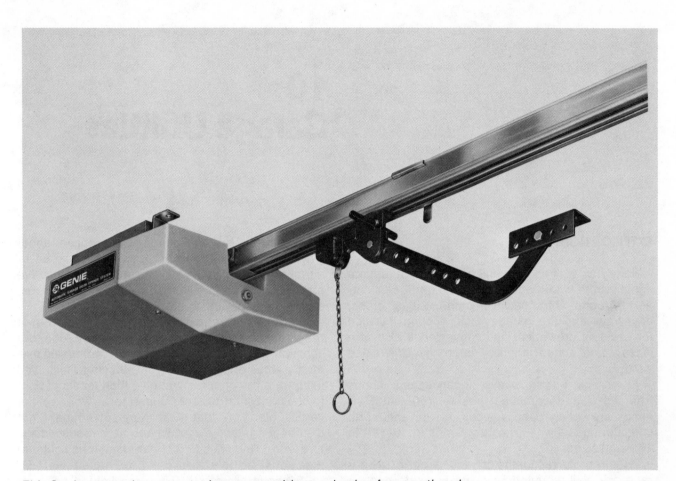

This Genie garage door operator has a screw-drive mechanism for smooth and quiet operation of both single and double, sectional and one-piece doors up to 7-feet 6-inches (2.1 meters, 152.4 mm) high. The compact unit has a digital control that provides up to 3000 codes. For added safety, it requires two depressions of the control button at approximately second-and-a-half intervals to activate closing. If the sequence of depressions is notably longer or shorter, activation will not take place and the operator must start all over again. (Photo courtesy of Alliance Manufacturing Co.)

10
Garage Utilities

EXTERIOR LIGHTING

Safety as well as convenience dictate adequate lighting both within and outside the garage or carport. Around entranceways, paths, walks, steps, driveways and the garage itself, lighting installed for accident prevention and convenience also provides a great added benefit by deterring prowlers and vandals.

At garage entranceways, incandescent lamps from 25-watt decorative types to 150-watt PAR lamps are widely used sources. Newer and worth considering are white mercury lamps in 50-watt to 175-watt sizes.

Usually preferred for the entrance areas of the garage are wall-mounted brackets in pairs, one on each side of the door. Effective mounting location is 5-1/2 feet (1.6 meters) above standing level. A single fixture, at the same height, is best located on the lock side of the door. It is also effective centered above the door. Good alternates are recessed units in the ceiling or roof overhang. Those fixtures are mounted higher above standing level and require higher-wattage lamps — at least 60-watt lamps for the side brackets, 75 or 100-watt lamps in the above-the-door fixtures.

General Electric lighting experts point out that while the design and scale of fixtures enhance the entrance appearance related to architecture, overall size should be no less than 50 square inches (322.5 square cm) luminous per fixture for lighting effectiveness. The luminous quality of fixtures is a factor often overlooked in favor of a "pretty" fixture.

Lighting fixtures used on the exterior of the garage often can be architecturally compatible for daytime viewing but bright and glaring at night. This problem is solved by correct shielding of the light source. Frosted or opal diffusing glasses are preferred. Clear glass is tolerable only when low-wattage lamps are used and the surrounding light level is fairly high.

In ceilings of roof overhangs or external entranceway structures such as breezeways, recessed or surface-mounted units can be installed. Effective size is 80 square inches (516 square cm) luminous, and in keeping with structural scale.

Although overhead units in most cases are out of the direct line of sight on approach, they require a light source shielding with some sort of diffusing material as their brightness can be annoying. Recessed fixtures, often unobtrusive, give high levels of light for the horizontal surfaces underfoot as well as in the vertical plane — that is, on a person's face. Light distribution is somewhat limited as a recessed fixture with 115 inches (2 921 mm) luminous lights an area equalling only about 6-1/2 to 7 square feet (.59 to .65 square meters). The area lighted by a recessed downlight with reflector lamp equals only about 4-1/2 to 5 feet square (.41 to .46 square meters). Thus, the best location for the single fixture is centered close to the entrance door.

Large areas can, of course, be lighted with multiple fixtures. Square fixtures are usually equipped with one 100-watt lamp, but some rectangular types with two lamp sockets offer better results. In either case, shielding with flat diffusing material or a lens plate is necessary.

Installations that incorporate both decorative wall-mounted fixtures and recessed functional lighting equipment often work best — the visible fixture's brightness and styling being for appearance, and the recessed equipment principally for light level necessary for seeing and safety.

Steps, paths and walks to and from the garage generally are illuminated by 25-watt to 150-watt incandescent lamps and white mercury lamps in the 50-watt to 175-watt range. The mercury units are more efficient and they have longer life to sustain safety and protection for greater periods between burnouts.

Various types of equipment are available for mounting above and below eye level to light ground areas. Ground-spike units and units with louvers or lens plate light distribution control are much used for walkways. Overhead units are available for tree or pole mountings. And there are post-top and wall-mounting lanterns designed for both decorative style and functional lighting.

Ground-lighting units installed below eye level normally light, at best, no more than an 8-foot (2.4 meters) diameter area, with the coverage influenced by size and shape of the reflector. Complete shielding of below-eye-level light sources is obviously necessary. When used along stairs, particular attention should be given to shielding because of possible low viewing angles. Spacings are generally considered effective if the semi-dark spaces between pools of light are not greater than the breadth of the light pools.

Louvered or lens plate type equipment designed for installation in walls adjoining paths are effective mounted between 16 and 25 inches (406.4 and 635 mm) above ground and not more than eight feet (2.4 meters) apart. They also are effective recessed in stair risers.

Post lanterns are effective lighting tools provided that styling design has not rendered them glaringly bright or restrictive in light distribution toward ground levels. Frosted glass diffusion, at least, is usually adequate; heavier diffusion materials are better. Prismatic lens control is best. It is an excellent light distribution feature.

A light distributing reflector built in above the lamp adds to its effectiveness depending upon the type of reflector. For styled wall-mounting units that serve functions similar to post lanterns, the same features apply. Post lanterns along paths and drives are most effective when spaced not more than 25 feet (7.6 meters) apart.

Overhead floodlighting from poles 10 to 20 feet (3 to 6 meters) high offers the advantage of widespread light distribution or sharp spot-beam control. Floodlighting lamps are effective in shields nine inches (228.6 mm) deep or more to hide the visible brightness of the lamps. Low voltage type lamps are another choice. They have built-in shielding that inhibits the spill light to control visible brightness.

Mercury vapor security lights with extending arms also are most suitable for garage-front illumination. These 175-watt fixtures have built-in ballast, are weatherproof and turn on at dusk, off at dawn.

The National Electrical Code and most local and state codes have provisions which are applicable to the installation of outdoor wiring. Compliance with these provisions follows the same pattern as with any other new or rewiring installation within the house. As a rule, most codes and ordinances covering fixed and portable equipment (lighting, tools, appliances), whether used indoors or outdoors, generally require that the equipment be electrically grounded. (See *Successful Home Electrical Wiring.*)

Electricity

All electricity used out of doors is supplied by two types of outlets: the permanently installed lighting fixture, and the permanently installed weatherproof outlet.

Outdoor lighting fixtures, whether post, wall or ceiling types, should be switch controlled from a convenient location inside the house, garage or both locations. The purpose of switch control (to furnish a pathway of light and provide convenience of control for this light) should determine the location of the switches. Therefore, switches should never be installed in a building away from the house or garage if this makes it necessary to walk in the dark to reach the switch locations.

Outdoor weatherproof outlets also should be switch controlled. Outlets used for power tools, barbecues and the like need not necessarily be switch controlled.

The National Electrical Code now requires all receptacles installed outdoors be GFI-protected (ground fault interrupter). Such devices fit standard 2-1/2-inch (63.5 mm) deep electrical wall boxes and shut off current immediately if the GFI senses a potentially hazardous flow of current to the ground, possibly through a person.

Several GFI models are available, including a receptacle kit developed by General Electric for the do-it-yourself market. This kit is designed to replace a standard 15 amp, 125 volt duplex receptacle and can be used in new construction or remodeling. The kit contains all materials and complete installation instructions.

INTERIOR LIGHTING

The minimum lighting requirement established for garage interiors is one lamp receptacle or fixture using one 100-watt bulb at each side of each parking area. The fixtures should be shielded to prevent glare and diffuse the illumination.

Use of three 100-watt fixtures so placed six feet (1.8 meters) from the back wall in a two-car garage

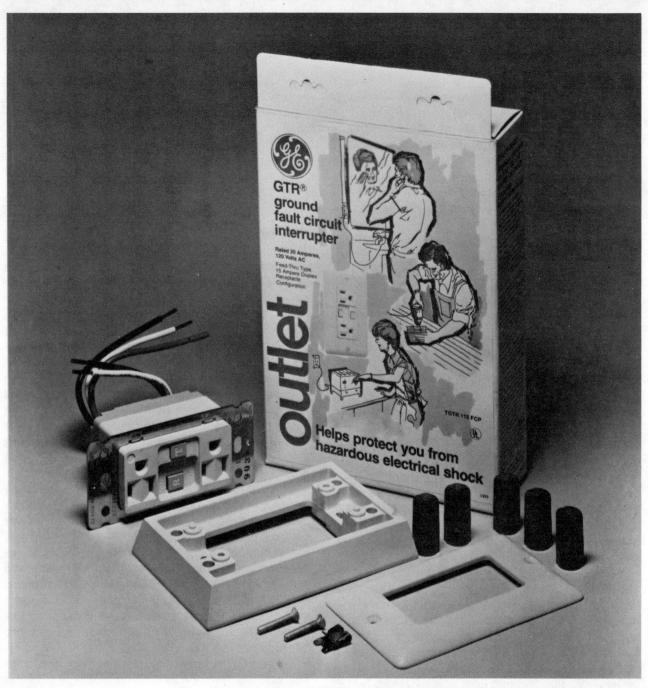

This GTR ground fault interrupter receptacle kit replaces a standard 15 amp. 125-volt duplex receptacle and protects against dangerous electric leaks which can occur without warning. (Photo courtesy of General Electric)

will provide good general lighting and will light up corners and sides where tools are stored, even when the cars are in the garage. Many homeowners, however, prefer to add still more lighting over workbenches or above areas where wood and metalworking power tools are used.

Fluorescent fixtures lamped with two 33-inch (838.2 mm) 25-watt tubes are recommended for use above workbenches. Such units should be positioned 48 inches (1 219.2 mm) above the work surface and at the front end of the bench if permanently installed. A better way is to purchase a fluorescent

fixture with extension cord and mount the unit at a 48-inch (1 219.2 mm) height on rods attached to the ceiling. This permits quick and easy movement of the fixture from the wall to the front of the bench and allows for exact placement for the tasks performed on the bench.

GFI-protected receptacles also are highly recommended for use in the garage and carport to eliminate the problem of dangerous moisture/power tool usage. As in the kitchen, electrical receptacles placed above workbench height are far more convenient than those installed low on the wall.

Garage workshops require concentrated illumination on the work surface. Here recessed fixtures provide glare-free lighting on the bench while a ceiling fixture (out of view) provides overall garage illumination. (Courtesy of Progress Lighting)

LAUNDRY FACILITIES

In warm climates, the garage or carport often doubles as the home laundry center, bringing about the need for additional utilities including cold and hot water supply, gas line, water drain and exhaust vents. Heating-air conditioning, hot water heater and water softener also are often installed here.

The in-line one-wall arrangement is the most efficient design for a garage or carport laundry. This needs a minimum nine feet (2.7 meters) of wall space sufficient for left-to-right placement of laundry tub, automatic washer and dryer, and a two-foot (.6 meters) base cabinet with countertop surface for folding items removed from the dryer.

Today's automatic washer requires a 115-volt, 60HZ electrical outlet and should have its own circuit. An electric dryer requires its own 230-volt, 60HZ three-wire circuit. Gas dryers require a 115-volt, 60HZ outlet which should be on a separate circuit from the washer. They may be operated with

either natural or LP gas, depending upon the dryer selection. Dryers should be located on exterior walls to minimize venting distance. Rigid aluminum or flexible plastic can be used for this purpose with the run not exceeding 50 feet (15.2 meters) from appliance to outdoors, less eight feet (2.4 meters) for each elbow that may be required.

The depth and height of regular-sized automatic washers are usually standard — up to 28 inches (711.2 mm) deep (add a few inches for clearance) and 43 inches high (1 092.2 mm). The width varies from 25 to 31 inches (635 to 787.4 mm). Compact automatic washers as narrow as 21 inches (533.4 mm) are available. Dryers range from 26 to 31 inches (660.4 to 787.4 mm) in width, from 42 to 45 inches (1,066.8 to 1 143 mm) in height and 25 to 31 inches (635 to 787.4 mm) in depth. Compact dryers are as small as 21 inches (533.4 mm) wide and 36 inches (914.4 mm) high.

Storage cabinets, shelves and bins for soiled and clean clothing should be a part of the garage/carport laundry center. Wall cabinets should be low enough for easy access to the shelves on which frequently used items are stored. Shelves should be adjustable. A minimum of three sorting bins is recommended for white clothes, colored items and a place for specials.

A clear space of 2-feet 6-inches (762 mm) should be provided in front of all appliances, workbenches, storage cabinets and around the automobile. For further safety, good ventilation should be provided with louvers and ceiling vents to carry off gasoline fumes, carbon monoxide and other chemical vapors. Where paints and chemicals are stored in closed cabinets, the door fronts should be the louvered type.

Rods attached to the ceiling permit easy movement and accurate positioning of a fluorescent fixture which should be 48 inches (1 219.2 mm) above the surface. This requires a fixture with extension cord and nearby outlet. (Sketch courtesy of General Electric)

11 Storage

A house hasn't been built that couldn't provide more storage space for its occupants — and this is certainly the situation regarding well-planned garage, carport and shed storage areas. In designing and building a new "place for the car," thoughtful consideration also should be given to increasing the value of the structure through inclusion of easily-accessible storage areas for other items. (See accompanying Checklist.)

Many homes constructed over the past several decades are without basements and attics, thus placing even more importance on valuable garage storage space. In these homes, it's often necessary to provide a storage system for luggage, infant equipment and temporarily out-of-use household items which in other homes are placed at rest above or below the living area.

As a basis for planning garage storage space, list all the items which will need storage. Decide where the items can be stored so they will be most convenient when they need to be used. Emphasis should be placed on maximum accessibility of all items stored, efficient use of space for storage, economy in construction and flexibility in the use of storage units. Safety from fire and injury also is a key factor.

Shelves are the most common and easy way to turn wasted space into working space in the garage. By standardizing shelving to three depths — 12 inches, 16 inches, and 24 inches (304.8, 406.4 and 609.6 mm) — it is possible to simplify construction and reduce costs.

Many materials are available for making shelves, commonly ranging from 1x12 (19x286 mm) pine to 1x4-inch (19x89 mm) pine, plywood, pre-cut parti-

Shelving brackets permit easily adjustable open storage on garage walls. The screw-attached metal standards accept click-in shelf brackets which can be located on 1-inch (25.4 mm) centers. Perforated hardboard panels are designed to store dozens of items. (Photo courtesy of Stanley Tool)

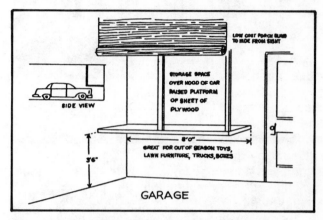

◄ *Among the many special brackets manufactured for garage wall storage is a full line of power tool brackets made for use with perforated hardboard. These brackets attach to either 1/8 or 1/4-inch (3.1 or 6.3 mm) panels and lock into place by means of a plastic locking pin. In addition to the power drill holder shown here, there are special brackets for sanders, jig saws, circular saws, hedge trimmers, and other devices for hand tools including hammers and screwdrivers. (Photo courtesy of ABL Associates, Inc.)*

Space over the hood of the car can be turned into valuable garage storage for out-of-season items. A roll-down porch shade can be used to keep items out of sight.

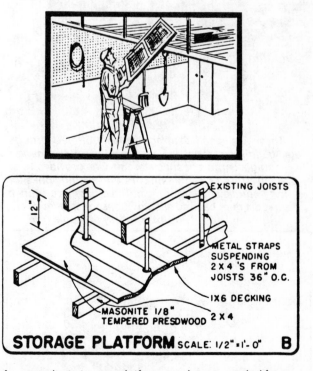

A convenient storage platform can be suspended from garage joists to provide a deck area for out-of-season window screens, storm windows and doors and other items. (Drawings courtesy of Masonite)

cleboard, hollow-core door slabs and lightweight open-wire units manufactured in a wide range of sizes. Shelf supports may be fabricated from wood or from any of a wide variety of steel and aluminum standards and brackets available at most building material outlets. Literally dozens of specific and multi-use hanging brackets also are available for direct attachment to wall studs or for instant relocation on walls surfaced with perforated hardboard.

Before planning your wall storage in the garage, give full consideration to the ceiling space and how it can be put to use for items not in frequent use. Open garage ceilings or even finished ceilings of sufficient height provide areas where platform storage can be utilized for luggage, Christmas decorations, out-of-season lawn furniture and the like.

If overhead space doesn't permit resting a platform on ceiling joists or suspending a platform from framing members, consider the construction of a partial platform suspended from the ceiling over just the hood of the car. This waste space can be further supported with 4x4-inch (89x89 mm) posts so placed as not to interfere with the in-out movement of the car.

Over-the-hood platform storage often can be as much as six feet (1.8 meters) in depth and in some garages can run the full width. Always use a full-size car in determining the size and height of this type storage. This will avoid any possibility of having to remove and rebuild at a later date or causing a "buyer" problem should you sell your home. Surface

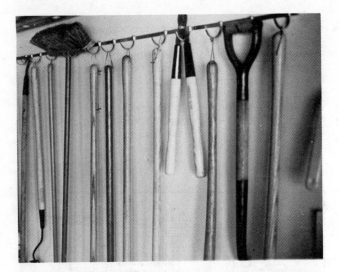

These two specific storage systems, offered through retail building material dealers, are intended to organize garage, carport or shed storage. One provides 16 or 32-inch (406.4 or 812.8 mm) bars with sliding hooks for long-handle and larger tools. The other has a 16-inch (406.4 mm) bar and sliding hooks for smaller items. (Photos courtesy of Stanley Works)

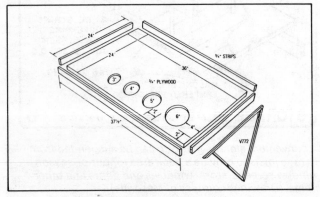

material should be 3/4-inch (19 mm) thickness for stability and maximum spans betweeen the supports.

By first planning your overhead platform storage, you can more accurately determine wall areas that will remain for providing cabinet, shelf and hanging storage. Generally, it's best to keep items raised several inches off the floor to prevent moisture problems and to permit easier floor cleaning as needed. A toe-space comparable to that used for your kitchen cabinets is sufficient.

Garages with unfinished walls, (studs are visible), provide still more space for wall storage. By using 1x4's (19x89 mm) between the studs you can create "in the wall" storage for paint cans, cleaners, canned foods and smaller-size items.

Stanley's hanging storage system is an excellent means of utilizing wall space most productively. Both 16 and 32-inch (406.4 and 812.8 mm) zinc-plated bars are designed for screw attachment to studs or wallboard and permit storage hooks to slide to any position on the bar. Heavy-duty storage hooks designed to support up to 50 pounds (22.6 kilograms) also are available to handle such items as snow tires, ladders, lawnmowers, wheelbarrows, sprayers, etc.

Still another popular way to create total garage wall storage flexibility is using floor-to-ceiling perforated hardboard (pegboard) sold by some retail outlets under the term "garage liner." These panels are 4-feet (1.2 meters) wide and are available for use with regular 1/8-inch (3.1 mm) perforated board fixtures or heavy-duty 1/4-inch (6.3 mm) self-locking fixtures. At least one wall of the heavy-duty board is recommended to handle such items as garden hose, sprayers, ladders and other heavy items. The smaller size fixtures are more adaptable to hand tools, sporting goods and the like.

Most residential garages serve double duty as the family workshop where general repairs may be made regardless of season, weather or time of the day. The convenience of a sturdy all-purpose workbench can be enjoyed by every member of the family old enough to tinker.

Home craftsmen have determined that a 32-1/2-inch (825.5 mm) base height plus 3/4-inch (19 mm) top surface is a most convenient height for woodworking, hobby and home repair work. The depth of the bench, if possible, should be 22 to 24 inches

◄ *This potting bench tucks neatly into a garage layout and folds out of the way when not in use. Metal folding brackets support the 3/4-inch (19 mm) plywood top which has cutouts for three, four, five and 6-inch (76.2, 101.6, 127 and 152.4 mm) diameter pots. (Drawing courtesy of Stanley Tools)*

A complete home workshop is a definite advantage of the over-sized garage. Full 4x8-foot (1.2x2.4 meters) Masonite Peg-Board has been used here for well-organized off-the-floor storage on walls, while the extended-length garage provides a workshop area. An alcove affords shelf storage space. Track lighting is in the work area while recessed fixtures are well spaced for over-all illumination without interfering with the overhead garage door and automatic garage door operator. (Photos by Matt Doherty)

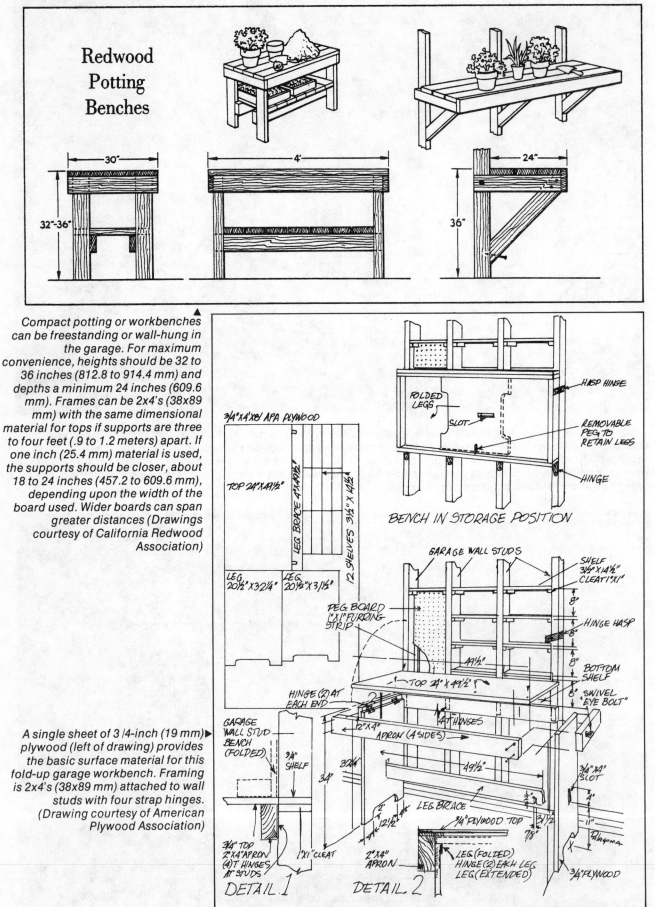

Redwood
Potting
Benches

Compact potting or workbenches can be freestanding or wall-hung in the garage. For maximum convenience, heights should be 32 to 36 inches (812.8 to 914.4 mm) and depths a minimum 24 inches (609.6 mm). Frames can be 2x4's (38x89 mm) with the same dimensional material for tops if supports are three to four feet (.9 to 1.2 meters) apart. If one inch (25.4 mm) material is used, the supports should be closer, about 18 to 24 inches (457.2 to 609.6 mm), depending upon the width of the board used. Wider boards can span greater distances (Drawings courtesy of California Redwood Association)

A single sheet of 3 /4-inch (19 mm) plywood (left of drawing) provides the basic surface material for this fold-up garage workbench. Framing is 2x4's (38x89 mm) attached to wall studs with four strap hinges. (Drawing courtesy of American Plywood Association)

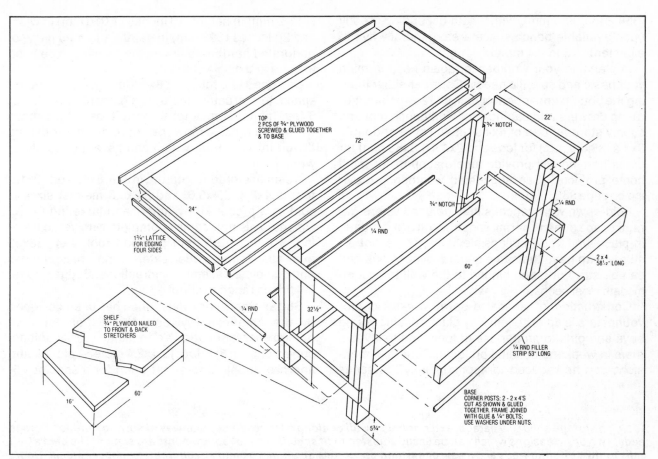

TOP
2 PCS OF ¾" PLYWOOD
SCREWED & GLUED TOGETHER
& TO BASE

72"

¾" NOTCH

22"

24"

¾" NOTCH

¼ RND

1¾" LATTICE
FOR EDGING
FOUR SIDES

¼ RND

60"

2 x 4
58½" LONG

SHELF
¾" PLYWOOD NAILED
TO FRONT & BACK
STRETCHERS

¼ RND

32½"

¼ RND FILLER
STRIP 53" LONG

16"

60"

5¾"

BASE
CORNER POSTS: 2 - 2 x 4'S
CUT AS SHOWN & GLUED
TOGETHER. FRAME JOINED
WITH GLUE & ¼" BOLTS;
USE WASHERS UNDER NUTS.

This basic workbench designed for use in the residential garage or basement has a 24x72-inch (609.6x1 828 mm) top surface constructed of two pieces of 3 /4-inch (19 mm) thick plywood. Full materials list and step-by-step construction plans are offered without charge. Refer to Manufacturer's List for address. (Drawing courtesy of Stanley Tools)

A scaled-down version of the adult workbench is designed for youngsters. Garage space required for this bench is 20x40 inches (508x1 016 mm). When the child grows taller, the bench still is a convenient height for numerous home workshop projects. (Photo courtesy of Stanley Tools)

(558.8 to 609.6 mm), with length depending greatly upon available bench space area, generally five to eight feet (1.5 to 2.4 meters) long.

In planning your workbench, again keep in mind your basic and specific needs. Consider either leaving the bottom area open for bulk storage or incorporating drawers and cabinets for workbench tool and supply storage. Use of 4x4's (89x89 mm) or double 2x4's (38x89 mm) for legs and 2x4's (38x89 mm) for cross framing will provide ample support for most home projects. (See suggested workbench drawing on page 93.)

Fold-down workbenches may be used where garage space doesn't permit construction of a full-time, in-place unit. The collapsible units, while not as sturdy, can have the same general dimensions and can be strap or piano hinged to the wall to accommodate most needs.

Construction of a scaled-down workbench for youngsters is an excellent way of introducing young boys and girls to proper use of tools and to involve them in weekend building projects. General dimensions can be reduced to approximately 28 inches

(711.2 mm) in height, 40 inches (1 016 mm) in width and 20 inches (508 mm) in depth. A framed piece of perforated hardboard above the bench can be used to store and display tools.

Designed to occupy an 8x12-foot (2.4x3.6 meters) space, this structure features a gambrel roof almost 8 feet high (2.4 meters) to permit maximum space within the area. A mower or garden tractor can be driven into the unit, which can have a concrete or wood floor.

A similar storage structure in 8x8, 8x12 and 12x12-foot (2.4x2.4, 2.4x3.6, and 3.6x3.6 meters) sizes is sold as a precut kit by American Marketing Corp., Omaha. This unit comes complete with vertical siding, 3/8-inch (9.5 mm) plywood roof, 2x4 (38x89 mm) stud frame, cedar exterior trim, nails, hinges and complete assembly instructions. Suggested retail prices range to about $600.

Still another "barn style" shed has been designed by the American Plywood Association for total homeowner fabrication and assembly. This unit occupies only an 8x8-foot (2.4x2.4 meters) plot of land and has double doors that open for a spacious 5-

Adding a storage shed to a garage, exterior house wall or along a fence is a popular way of solving outdoor storage needs. Two basic designs which can be easily adjusted to fit specific space requirements are shown. The plan at left calls for two existing walls and a new or existing concrete slab upon which to attach treated lumber mudsill. Doors can be either swing or slide-type, depending upon finish dimensions and preferences. The shed design at right can be used where only a single wall exists by adding a 2x6 (38x140 mm) pole constructed as a free-standing unit. Recommended rafter sizes are 2x6's (38x140 mm) in snow areas and 2x4's (38x89 mm) elsewhere, located on 16 or 24-inch (406.4 or 609.6 mm) centers. (Drawings courtesy of Western Wood Products Association)

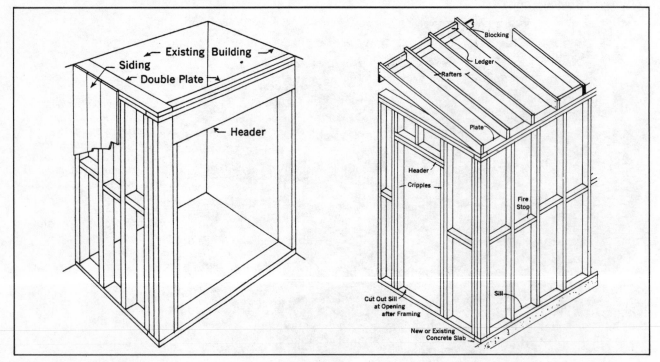

foot-wide (1.5 meters) entry, providing plenty of room to wheel equipment in without having to forge through a clutter of tools. Extra storage space is available by simply nailing 2x4's (38x89 mm) to the inside walls and installing hooks or metal angle brackets and shelves.

The APA barn requires four panels of 1/2-inch (12.7 mm) exterior plywood, six panels of Texture 1-11 siding, lumber for framing, roof shingles, hardware, and paint or stain for finishing. Construction is easy because wall and roof sections are completed separately and then fastened together.

Extremely popular in western areas has been the Stow-It-All storage fence designed by Western Wood Products Association. Built of separate three-foot (.9 meters) modules, you just add another unit and attach it as your storage needs increase. The initial unit is comprised of five modules set side by side on a 4x8 (1.2x2.4 meters) or nail-laminated 2x8 (.6x2.4 meters) pressure treated foundation. Construction is of 1x8 (19x184 mm) and 1x4 (19x89 mm) western wood boards and framing.

Building materials dealers throughout the United States offer homeowners a selection of prefab metal storage houses, with or without plywood floors, for assembly in less than a day. These aluminum and steel frame structures incorporate a series of overlapping wall and roof panels for weathertightness and usually have double sliding doors that glide on inside tracks to afford maximum accessibility.

Prefab metal building sizes range from 6x5-foot (1.8x1.5 meters) to 12x10-foot (3.6x3 meters) with designs including a selection of roof treatments, vinyl woodgrain exterior finishes, built-in entry ramps, translucent sunroof panels, and decorative trim. A solid foundation is recommended and may be concrete, brick, cement block or treated lumber. Most units provide a 6-foot (1.8 meters) walk-in area and peaks ranging up to 7-plus feet (2.1 meters) to prevent bumping your head. Shelves can be used for smaller objects to free valuable floor space for more bulky items and wheel equipment.

More customized storage sheds can be designed to serve multi functions such as a unit doubling as a storage shelter-cabana adjacent to a swimming pool. Again, plans are available from the American Plywood Association for a four-foot-square (.37 square meters) and 7-1/2-foot high (2.2 meters) mansard-roofed unit that's easy and inexpensive to build and maintain.

Framed with 2x2's (38x38 mm) and 2x4's (38x89 mm), this shelter is sided with 3/8-inch (9.5 mm) rough sawn siding that can be stained to harmonize with house and fence. A sheet of 3/8-inch (9.5 mm) C-C plugged and touch-sanded exterior plywood is used to divide the changing room and the storage cupboard. A 27-inch (685.5 mm) square of 1/4-inch (6.3 mm) Plexiglass or other transparent thermoplastic serves as a skylight in the dressing area.

Storage walls can be added to existing carports or planned as part of the initial construction. Length depends upon the distance between supports, or new 4x4 (89x89 mm) corner support columns can be added to open the entire length to storage purposes. This plan is based on use of a 4-foot (1.2 meters) module with depths of 16, 24 or 32 inches (406.4, 609.6 or 812.8 mm). (Drawing courtesy of American Plywood Association. See Manufacturer's List for address.)

GARAGE STORAGE CHECKLIST

Few persons realize the tremendous number of items commonly stored in the garage. Listed here are the most-often mentioned by homeowners, who participated in a national design program conducted by Owens-Corning Fiberglas.

1. **VEHICLES**
   Automobiles, tires, tools, cleaning equipment, etc.
   Bicycles, tools, tires.
   Boats, motorcycles, mopeds, etc.
   Baby carriages, strollers.

2. **OUTDOOR GAMES**
   Nets, posts, wickets, bags, gloves, rackets, mallets, bats,
   balls, clubs, golf bags, skates, skis, outboard motors,
   plastic swimming pools, hockey sets, hunting and fishing equipment,
   scuba equipment, water skis.

3. **GARDEN TOOLS**
   Wheelbarrows, spray trucks, rollers, lawn mowers, edgers, leaf
   blowers, chain saws, fertilizer spreaders, snow blowers.
   Hoses, string, stakes, flower pots, seeds, sprays, fertilizer.
   Clippers, pruner, gloves, hoes, rakes, shovels, forks, lawn sweeper.

4. **HOME IMPROVEMENT ITEMS**
   Ladders.
   Paints and sundries.
   Woodworking and metalworking power and hand tools.
   Nails, fasteners and repair items.
   Lumber, plywood, plastics.

5. **INDOOR GAMES**
   Ping-pong tables, other table games.

6. **GARDEN AND PORCH FURNITURE**
   Chairs, tables, chaise lounge.
   Swings, hammocks.
   Barbecue and barbecue accessories.

7. **WINTERIZING/SUMMERIZING EQUIPMENT**
   Screens, screen doors, storm sash and storm doors.
   Snow removal gear, boots, snow shovels.

8. **WASTE**
   Waste paper storage.
   Garbage storage.
   Outdoor-waste storage, leaves, garden refuse, etc.

9. **POISONS**
   Garden insecticides.
   Ammonia, spot removers, disinfectants, bleaches, drain solvent.

10. **FUEL**
    Wood, paper, kindling.
    Oil, bottled gas.
    Charcoal, gasoline.

11. **YOU ADD TO LIST**
    All things large and small that you can't bring yourself to part with.

12
Storage Sheds

With more and more emphasis being placed on the use of leisure time around the home plus the growing incidence of two or more cars per family, the demand for outdoor shed storage space has never been greater.

Today's family, regardless of size, has far more items to protect from the elements than generations of the past. There's everything from basic lawn furniture to pool and hot tub equipment and supplies, and at the same time, less and less space in the garage to accomodate such items.

Building a storage shed in most communities, like building a new garage or carport, requires a permit from the local government, following acceptance of construction plans. In some communities, such buildings are not permitted so it is well to check this point before incurring any expense. Again, like building a garage, you'll need lot line dimensions and a

This shed was designed to house a bandsaw, belt sander, jigsaw, jointer, and dozens of accessories. The shed stands 96-inches (2 4384 mm) long, 33-inches (838.2 mm) deep and 54-inches (1 371.6 mm) high at the front and 50-inches (1 270 mm) at the rear.   (Plan courtesy of Shopsmith)

Called the Stow-It-All, this storage fence will accommodate all your bulky outdoor yard equipment. The unit is built of separate three-foot (.9 meters) modules to permit easy expansion as needed and utilizes the fence as the rear wall surface. The floor can be gravel, concrete or 1x4's (19x89 mm) supported by treated 4x6's (89x140 mm). Door interiors have shelves for maximum storage usage. (Photo courtesy of Western Wood Products Association)

scale plan of all existing buildings on your property as well as the intended location of the storage shed, with adjoining set-back and side-line dimensions noted.

In some communities where building a permanent outdoor shed is not permitted, the local building code will allow temporary, factory-made units sold by local building material dealers in KD (knockdown) or assembled form. These retail outlets usually can advise you of local acceptance, but it's best to check this point before making the purchase.

One of the most popular prefab storage buildings

More formal storage sheds can provide additional uses such as backyard home entertaining. This model has painted bevel cedar siding and an attractive screen-gate combination which partially hides the service yard at the rear of the structure. A standard concrete slab was used under the building while exposed aggregate trimmed with brick was used for the approach and patio area. (Photo courtesy of Western Wood Products Association)

This 8x10 (2.4x3 meters) tool house utilizes standard aluminum building panels for roof and sidewalls and readily-available dimensional lumber for the framework. Concrete or pressure treated wood can be used for the floor and 8x8x16-inch (200x200x400 mm) concrete blocks eliminate the need for special footings. Aluminum can be cut with a fine tooth sabre saw or portable circular saw. (Drawings courtesy of Reynolds Aluminum)

(especially in the Midwest) is the little red barn storage building. (See page 115.) Supplies are available at most building material outlets.

Designed to occupy an 8x12-foot (2.4x3.6 meters) space, this structure features a gambrel roof almost 8 feet high (2.4 meters) to permit maximum space within the area. A mower or garden tractor can be driven into the unit, which can have a concrete or wood floor.

A similar storage structure in 8x8, 8x12 and 12x12-foot (2.4x2.4, 2.4x3.6, and 3.6x3.6 meters) sizes is sold as a precut kit by American Marketing Corp., Omaha. This unit comes complete with verti-

cal siding, 3/8-inch (9.5 mm) plywood roof, 2x4 (38x89 mm) stud frame, cedar exterior trim, nails, hinges and complete assembly instructions. Suggested retail prices range to about $600.

Still another "barn style" shed has been designed by the American Plywood Association for total homeowner fabrication and assembly. This unit occupies only an 8x8-foot (2.4x2.4 meters) plot of land and has double doors that open for a spacious 5-foot-wide (1.5 meters) entry, providing plenty of room to wheel equipment in without having to forge through a clutter of tools. Extra storage space is available by simply nailing 2x4's (38x89 mm) to the inside walls and installing hooks or metal angle brackets and shelves.

The APA barn requires four panels of 1/2-inch (12.7 mm) exterior plywood, six panels of Texture 1-11 siding, lumber for framing, roof shingles, hardware, and paint or stain for finishing. Construction is easy because wall and roof sections are completed separately and then fastened together.

Extremely popular in western areas has been the Stow-It-All storage fence designed by Western Wood Products Association. Built of separate three-foot (.9 meters) modules, you just add another unit and attach it as your storage needs increase. The initial unit is comprised of five modules set side by side on a 4x8 (1.2x2.4 meters) or nail-laminated 2x8 (.6x2.4 meters) pressure treated foundation. Con-

Texture 1-11 plywood and perforated tempered hardboard are the key materials used for this open-air style table storage shed. Building dimensions are four feet (1.2 meters) deep by 16 feet (4.8 meters) long with a larger roof providing weather protection. This unit has had favor in warm climates where snow and excessive rain are not problems. (Photo courtesy of Georgia-Pacific)

This poolside /garden storage shed required only 32 square feet (2.9 square meters) of ground space (8x4 feet or 2.4x1.2 meters) and has a 6-foot 8-inch (1.8 meters, 203. 2 mm) front height sloping to 4-feet 6-inches (1.2 meters, 152.4 mm) at the rear. Constructed of 3 /8-inch (9.5 mm) rough sawn plywood, the structure has 2x2 (38x38 mm) and 2x4 (38x89 mm) framing. Bottom sills are redwood or treated lumber which permits the unit to be placed on a concrete deck or bed of gravel. Material costs are held to a minimum. For example, plywood requirements come to eight 4x8 (1.2x2.4 meters) panels which, when cut, also leave material for shelving. (Photo courtesy of the American Plywood Association)

struction is of 1x8 (19x184 mm) and 1x4 (19x89 mm) western wood boards and framing.

Building materials dealers throughout the United States offer homeowners a selection of prefab metal storage houses, with or without plywood floors, for assembly in less than a day. These aluminum and steel frame structures incorporate a series of overlapping wall and roof panels for weathertightness and usually have double sliding doors that glide on inside tracks to afford maximum accessibility.

Prefab metal building sizes range from 6x5-foot (1.8x1.5 meters) to 12x10-foot (3.6x3 meters) with designs including a selection of roof treatments, vinyl woodgrain exterior finishes, built-in entry ramps, translucent sunroof panels, and decorative trim. A solid foundation is recommended and may be concrete, brick, cement block or treated lumber. Most units provide a 6-foot (1.8 meters) walk-in area and peaks ranging up to 7-plus feet (2.1 meters) to prevent bumping your head. Shelves can be used for smaller objects to free valuable floor space for more bulky items and wheel equipment.

More customized storage sheds can be designed to serve multi functions such as a unit doubling as a storage shelter-cabana adjacent to a swimming pool. Again, plans are available from the American Plywood Association for a four-foot-square (.37 square meters) and 7-1/2-foot high (2.2 meters) mansard-roofed unit that's easy and inexpensive to build and maintain.

Double sliding doors permit easy drive-in storage of a small lawn mower in this Buckingham model prefab metal storage house. Translucent roof panels provide full daytime visibility without need for electrical lighting. A 4-inch (101.6 mm) perimeter shelf includes convenient tool holders. (Drawing courtesy of Arrow Group Industries, Inc.)

This Kensington model storage house has a galvanized steel foundation, plus steel framing for long-time usage. The unit has sliding interior doors that glide on a permanently lubricated track. It also has handles which can be padlocked. (Drawing courtesy of Arrow Group Industries, Inc.)

Framed with 2x2's (38x38 mm) and 2x4's (38x89 mm), this shelter is sided with 3/8-inch (9.5 mm) rough sawn siding that can be stained to harmonize with house and fence. A sheet of 3/8-inch (9.5 mm) C-C plugged and touch-sanded exterior plywood is used to divide the changing room and the storage cupboard. A 27-inch (685.8 mm) square of 1/4-inch (6.3 mm) Plexiglass or other transparent thermoplastic serves as a skylight in the dressing area.

This cut-away illustration demonstrates the potential use of steel storage sheds sold by retail building material dealers. This model can be used on a concrete slab or have a plywood floor, as desired. (Drawing courtesy of Arrow Group Industries, Inc.)

13
Projects with Plans for Building

THE POLE TYPE GARAGE 24′x24′ (7.3x7.3 meters)

One of the most economical ways to build a garage or storage building is to copy the farmer's modern pole barn. Building codes permitting, this type of construction eliminates the need for a foundation and even the floor can be omitted, if desired. Larger buildings of this type can be built but the sizes of members will increase. *See Farm Builders Handbook,* third edition by R.J. Lytle, et al.

Either pressure treated posts (4x4 or 89x89 mm) or poles (4-inch or 101.6 mm top) can be used. These are set in the ground in normal soil, 42-inches (1 066.8 mm) deep for the post or 52-inches (1 320.8 mm) for the pole. In soft or unstable soil, go 12-inches (304.8 mm) deeper. Drill holes with a rented drill. Using pre-mixed concrete in bags, mix some concrete fairly dry and put about six-inches (152.4 mm) in the bottom of each hole. Set and align the poles while the concrete is still damp. Backfill the holes, preferably with gravel, and tamp (pack down tightly).

The roof trusses can be made using the regular size "Truss Pack" manufactured by The Panel Clip Co. Follow the drawing which calls for a 2x6 (38x140 mm) top chord and 2x4 (38x89 mm) bottom.

Build the trusses carefully, according to instructions, with lumber cut exactly. Install two 2x4 (38x89 mm) braces (not shown) from the peak of the second truss away from the gable end, to the bottom of the gable end. Then run a 1x6 (19x140 mm) or 2x4 (38x89 mm) tie across the tops of the 2x4 (38x89 mm) bottom chords from gable to gable, nailing to each truss.

The 2x6 (38x140 mm) plate on which the trusses bear should be nailed to each post or pole with 20d galvanized barn spikes, three at each post. The anchor clip, used to anchor the truss to the pole, also is a Panel Clip product.

The drawing shows a maximum 10-foot (3 meters) eave height but you may wish to make your garage less than this.

Follow the construction details shown. Metal siding and roofing, steel or aluminum, can be used. A variation is to substitute some fiberglass panels on the roof, with the same corrugations as the metal, for skylights.

Be sure to brace the corners as shown. Installing one or more pieces of pressure treated 2x6 or 2x8 (38x140 mm or 38x184 mm) at the ground level will keep the metal away from the ground and provide a form for concrete.

Plans courtesy of The Panel Clip Co.

EAVE TRIM & GABLE EDGE TRIM

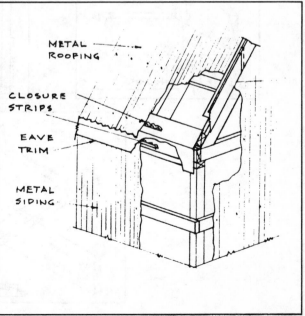

METAL ROOFING

CLOSURE STRIPS

EAVE TRIM

METAL SIDING

THE POLE TYPE GARAGE

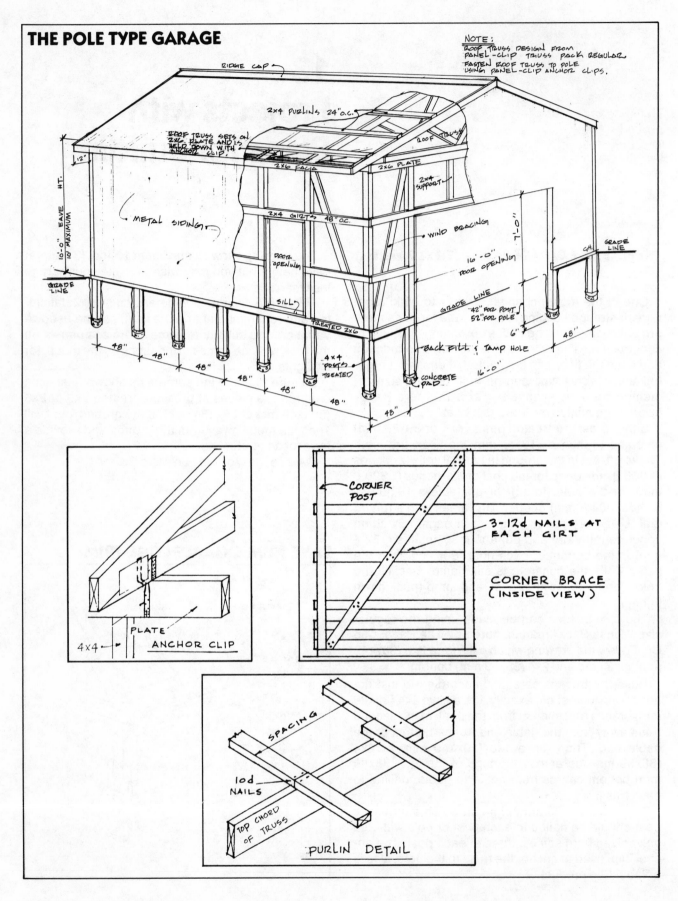

NOTE:
ROOF TRUSS DESIGN FROM
PANEL-CLIP TRUSS PACK REGULAR.
FASTEN ROOF TRUSS TO POLE
USING PANEL-CLIP ANCHOR CLIPS.

RIDGE CAP

2x4 PURLINS 24" O.C.

ROOF TRUSS SETS ON 2x6 PLATE AND IS HELD DOWN WITH ANCHOR CLIP.

ROOF TRUSS

2x6 FASCIA

2x6 PLATE

2x4 SUPPORT

12"

METAL SIDING

2x4 GIRTS 48" O.C.

WIND BRACING

7'-0"

GRADE LINE

16'-0" EAVE HT.
16' MAXIMUM

DOOR OPENING

16'-0" DOOR OPENING

GRADE LINE

GRADE LINE

SILL

TREATED 2x6

GRADE LINE

42" FOR POST
52" FOR POLE

BACK FILL & TAMP HOLE

6"

48"

48"

48"

48"

48"

48"

48"

48"

4x4 POSTS TREATED

CONCRETE PAD

16'-0"

CORNER POST

3-12d NAILS AT EACH GIRT

CORNER BRACE
(INSIDE VIEW)

4x4

PLATE

ANCHOR CLIP

SPACING

10d NAILS

TOP CHORD OF TRUSS

PURLIN DETAIL

THE TWO-CAR GARAGE

The primary function of a garage is to provide shelter and security for your automobile. But the fact is that the family garage has become a building with a multitude of uses. A garage can be used as an all-around storage building for house and garden tools and other similar equipment. A garage is even a good place to work when using power tools for do-it-yourself home projects. It provides better circulation when cutting or sanding than does a basement workshop, for example, and you keep the sawdust out of the house. (Plans courtesy of the Panel Clip Co.)

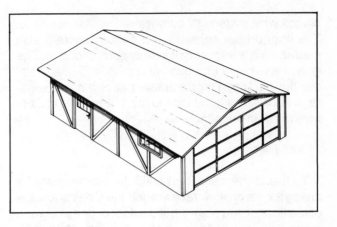

Laying the Concrete Floor

The first job is to lay out the ground for the 20-foot x 24-foot concrete slab floor (Fig. A). The ground must be cleared and leveled; then the forms for the floor are put together. Footings 16-inches thick and 12-inches wide are poured along both sides and the back of the floor. Twenty Anchor Clips are set in the footings, six along each side, six on the back and two in the front. Be sure to anchor the baseplates in

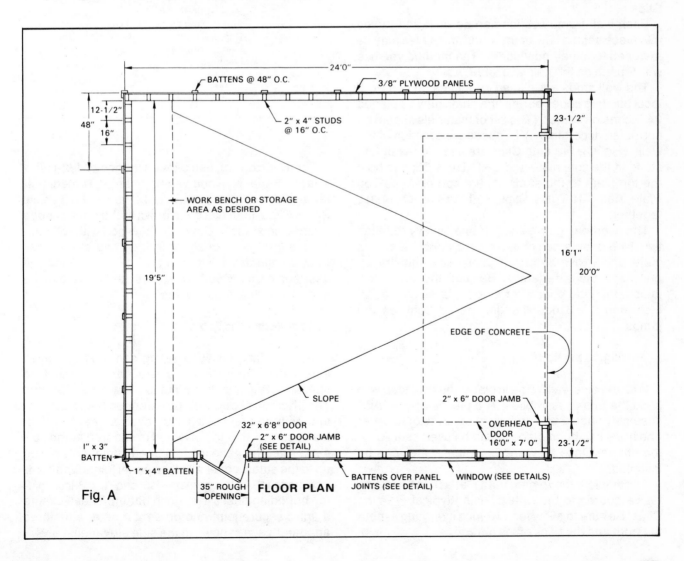

Fig. A   FLOOR PLAN

places where studs or corners will not be nailed in. The floor proper consists of a 4-inch concrete slab poured on a 5-inch bed of evenly spread gravel. The gravel ensures a firm base and proper drainage under the garage. To guarantee a strong durable garage floor, it is a good idea to lay 3/8-inch tie rods or wire mesh in the concrete.

Wall Framing

To frame the walls, first build the bottom plate by laying 2 x 4's on their face around the sides and back of the floor. If you plan to build a door in one side wall, leave a 35-inch wide opening at the correct position in the bottom plate for the door and two door jambs. Also cut two pieces of 2 x 4, each 18-1/2-inches long, and lay these at the front of the floor, butting against the 2 x 4 bottom plate at the sides (Figs. A and B). The entire base or sole plate is fastened down to the concrete floor by means of the Anchor Clips.

Each wall frame section can be built and raised into place separately, or the studs and plates may be fastened together individually. The method you use will depend on the help available.

The wall studs are placed 16-inches on center. If local building codes permit, the studs may be placed 24-inches on center. (The list of materials should be corrected accordingly.) To speed the erection of the walls (Fig. C), Framing Clips are used to fasten the studs to the sole plate and 2 HD Truss Clips to hold the top plate to the studs. At the corners, use Top Plate Ties (4H Truss Clips) to hold the top plates together.

The overhead garage door frame usually requires two 2 x 6 door jambs on the side, a double 2 x 4 top plate, and an overhead 2 x 6 jamb nailed into the top plate and the side jambs. Besides the two 2 x 6 jambs, the side doorway frame requires only a 32-inch long 2 x 6 door header, nailed between the jambs.

Putting on the Roof

With the side wall frame in place, the next step is to build the truss assemblies. The pieces of one truss assembly should be carefully measured for fit. After one truss has been made, it can be used as a jig for the others. Once they are assembled, they can be installed.

To complete the roofing frame, attach the two side fascia boards to the rafters, using typical Framing Clips. Be sure to allow for a 16-inch overhang at both the front and the back of the garage.

MATERIALS

Quantity	Description
21	3/8" x 4' x 8' Exterior siding panels for walls
21	3/8" x 4' x 8' Exterior fir plywood panels for roof
16 lin. feet	1" x 2" Trim
32 lin. feet	1" x 3" Corner battens
208 lin. feet	1" x 4" Siding and corner battens
600 lin. feet	2" x 4" Studs and plates
72 lin. feet	2" x 6" Door jambs and window sill, fascia
Truss lumber:	Top and bottom chord members: (39) 2" x 4" - 12' and (13) 2" x 4" - 8' Web members: 195 lin. feet
1	16' x 6'8" Exterior door (style as desired)
1	Window (height as desired)
27 lin. feet	Ridge cap
4	Panel-Clip Truss Packs—Regular Span
161	Panel-Clip Framing Clips
4	Panel-Clip Single Purlin Clips 2" x 4"
26	Panel-Clip Saddle Purlin Clips 2" x 4"
28	Panel-Clip Anchor Clips 14-3/4" length
60	Panel-Clip Panel Clips 3/8" size
26	Panel-Clip Storm Clips
—	Panel-Clip Nails
—	Roll roofing material
—	Hardware for side and overhead doors
—	Galvanized nails
—	Flashing
—	Concrete
—	Gravel
—	Paint or stain

For a sturdy roof, use either 3/8-inch or 1/2-inch x 4-feet x 8-feet plywood panels or an equivalent material. Connect the panels with Panel-Clip Typical Panel Clips, then nail them down to the rafters, ridge boards, and fascia. Cover the plywood with roll roofing material and construct a ridge cap at the peak from aluminum or two strips of 1-inch x 3-inch. If desired, either wood or asphalt shingles can be added as a final touch on the roof.

Completing the Job

The 3/8-inch plywood siding can next be nailed into place. The 4-feet x 8-feet panels should be spaced 1/8-inch at the joints to allow for expansion. The plywood should also be extended below the bottom plate to provide a 1-inch overhang at the slab. Make certain that the plywood is squared at the corners. After the paneling has been completely nailed up to the studs, cover all of the panel joints with 1 x 4-inch battens. At the corners use one 1 x 3-inch batten butted against a 1 x 4-inch batten. These ensure a tight, secure joint and present a neat, structured appearance, as shown in the side elevations.

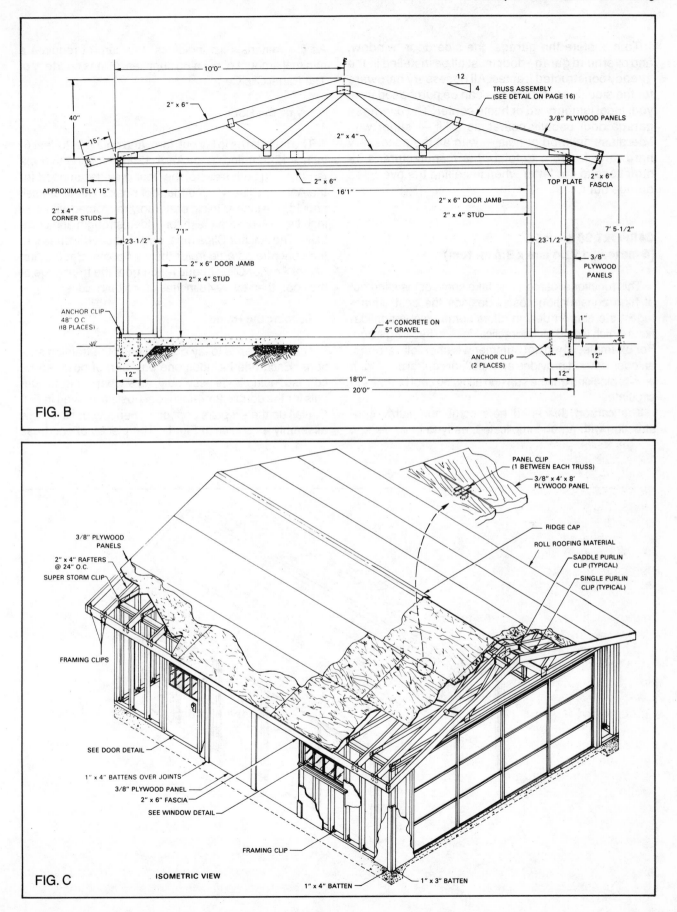

10'0"

40"

15"

2" x 6"

2" x 4"

TRUSS ASSEMBLY
(SEE DETAIL ON PAGE 16)

12
4

3/8" PLYWOOD PANELS

APPROXIMATELY 15"

2" x 4"
CORNER STUDS

23-1/2"

7'1"

2" x 6"

16'1"

2" x 6" DOOR JAMB
2" x 4" STUD

TOP PLATE

2" x 6"
FASCIA

7' 5-1/2"

2" x 6" DOOR JAMB
2" x 4" STUD

23-1/2"

3/8"
PLYWOOD
PANELS

ANCHOR CLIP
48" O.C.
(18 PLACES)

4" CONCRETE ON
5" GRAVEL

1"

12"

ANCHOR CLIP
(2 PLACES)

4"

12"

18'0"

12"

12"

20'0"

FIG. B

PANEL CLIP
(1 BETWEEN EACH TRUSS)

3/8" x 4' x 8'
PLYWOOD PANEL

3/8" PLYWOOD
PANELS

2" x 4" RAFTERS
@ 24" O.C.

SUPER STORM CLIP

RIDGE CAP

ROLL ROOFING MATERIAL

SADDLE PURLIN
CLIP (TYPICAL)

SINGLE PURLIN
CLIP (TYPICAL)

FRAMING CLIPS

SEE DOOR DETAIL

1" x 4" BATTENS OVER JOINTS

3/8" PLYWOOD PANEL

2" x 6" FASCIA

SEE WINDOW DETAIL

FRAMING CLIP

FIG. C   **ISOMETRIC VIEW**

1" x 4" BATTEN

1" x 3" BATTEN

To complete the garage, the side door, window, and overhead garage door must all be installed in the already constructed frames. All necessary hardware for the side door and window can be purchased from your local lumberyard or home center. The overhead garage door usually comes as a kit — either with fiberglass or wood panels — with all the necessary hardware. Be sure to follow the manufacturer's instructions to the letter when installing the overhead garage door.

CARPORT 20′6′′ x 12′
(6 meters, 152.4 mm x 3.6 meters)

This functional carport can take some of the sting out of high construction costs. Besides the cost advantages, the carport design offers some unique applications which would be impractical for a full-scale garage. For example, when hot summer weather rolls around, an open carport provides an excellent central point for a picnic, blocking out the sun and allowing cool breezes to circulate.

The carport described here combines sturdy construction with an uncomplicated, easy-to-build design.

As the materials list indicates, the carport requires a minimal amount of building supplies. (Plans courtesy of The Panel Clip Co.)

Laying the Floor

The first step is to lay out, form and pour the 20-feet 6-inch x 12-feet floor (Fig. A). A 12-inch footing that extends along both sides of the floor provides support for the Anchor Clips holding the roof posts. The floor itself should be 4 inches thick, preferably reinforced with 3/8-inch tie rods or wire mesh for added strength and durability. The Anchor Clips must be set about 8-inches into the concrete as a tie-in for the roof posts. Set the first pair of Anchor Clips about 1-inch from the front edge of the floor, then every 48 inches along both sides.

Building the Frame

The next step is to lay out and build the framing sections. Each one includes one pair of roof posts and a corresponding truss assembly, as shown in Fig. B. Details for the double 2 x 4-inch roof posts are given in Fig. C. Nail up the six pairs of posts. Then, lay out the truss assembly as shown in Fig. D. The pieces of one truss

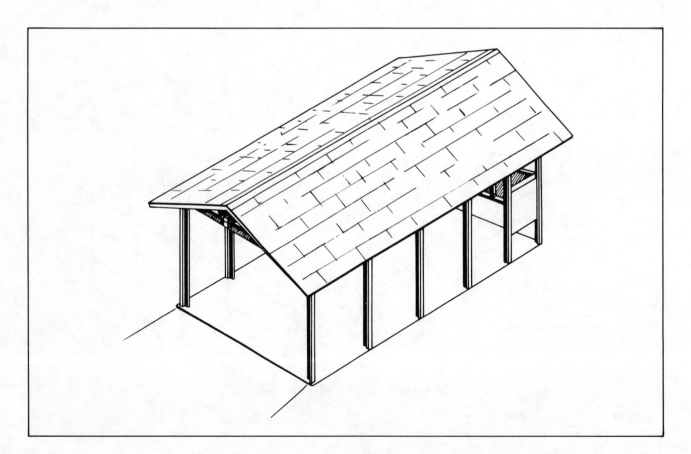

MATERIALS

Quantity	Description
12	5/8" x 4' x 8' Exterior fir plywood roof panels
3	1/4" x 4' x 8' Exterior fir plywood panels for bracing screen
634 lin. feet	2" x 4" Posts, fascia, blocking, purlins, rafters, etc.
96 lin. feet	2" x 3" Bracing screen frame
20 lin. feet	1" x 6" Cedar cap for bracing screen
24 lin. feet	Ridge molding
12	Panel-Clip 22-3/4" Anchor Clips
28	Panel-Clip Framing Clips
12	Panel-Clip 2" x 4" Saddle Purlin Clips
4	Panel-Clip 2" x 4" Single Purlin Clips
12	Panel-Clip Regular Storm Clips
28	Panel-Clip 5/8" Panel Clips
2 pkgs.	Truss Pack—Regular Span
—	Panel-Clip Nails
—	Roll roofing material
—	Galvanized nails
—	Paint or stain
—	Concrete

CARPORT PLAN (POST SETTING)

FIG. A

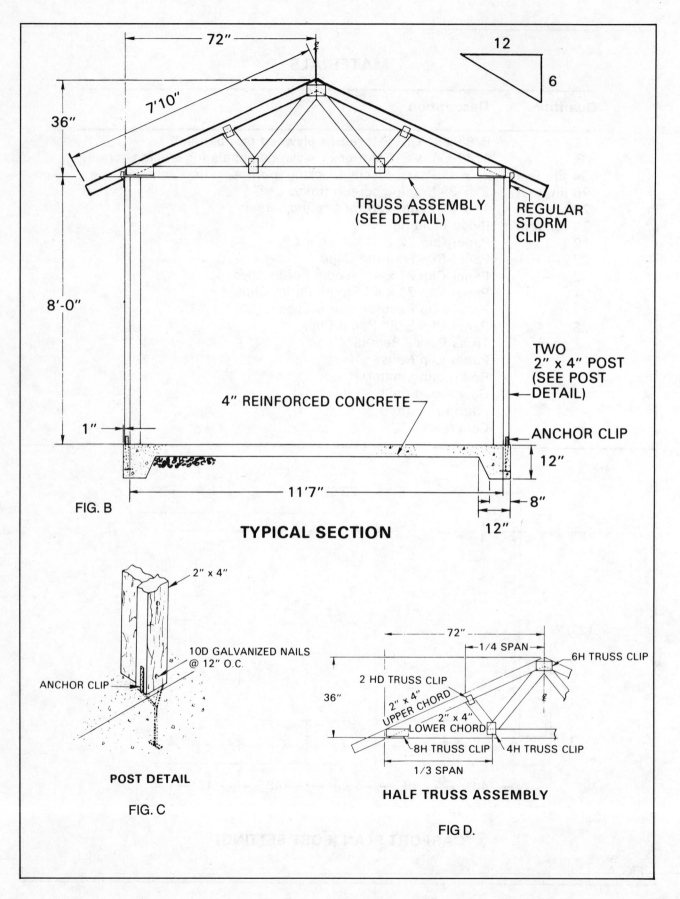

72"

7'10"

36"

12

6

TRUSS ASSEMBLY
(SEE DETAIL)

REGULAR
STORM
CLIP

8'-0"

TWO
2" x 4" POST
(SEE POST
DETAIL)

4" REINFORCED CONCRETE

ANCHOR CLIP

1"

12"

11'7"

8"

FIG. B

12"

TYPICAL SECTION

2" x 4"

10D GALVANIZED NAILS
@ 12" O.C.

ANCHOR CLIP

POST DETAIL

FIG. C

72"

1/4 SPAN

6H TRUSS CLIP

2 HD TRUSS CLIP

36"

2" x 4"
UPPER CHORD

2" x 4"
LOWER CHORD

8H TRUSS CLIP

4H TRUSS CLIP

1/3 SPAN

HALF TRUSS ASSEMBLY

FIG D.

assembly should be carefully measured for fit. After one truss has been made, it can be used as a jig for the others. Fasten the truss assemblies to the roof post, using regular Storm Clips.

Framing

The framing sections are erected one at a time. Once the posts are in place, they are attached to the Anchor Clips; the framing may be held in place, if necessary, by temporary bracing.

Putting On the Roof

For a sturdy roof, use 5/8-inch x 4-feet x 8-feet plywood or an equivalent material (Fig. E). Connect the panels with Panel Clips, then nail them down to the rafters, ridge boards, and fascia. Cover the plywood with roll roofing material and construct a ridge cap at the peak from aluminum or two strips of 1 x 3 lumber. If

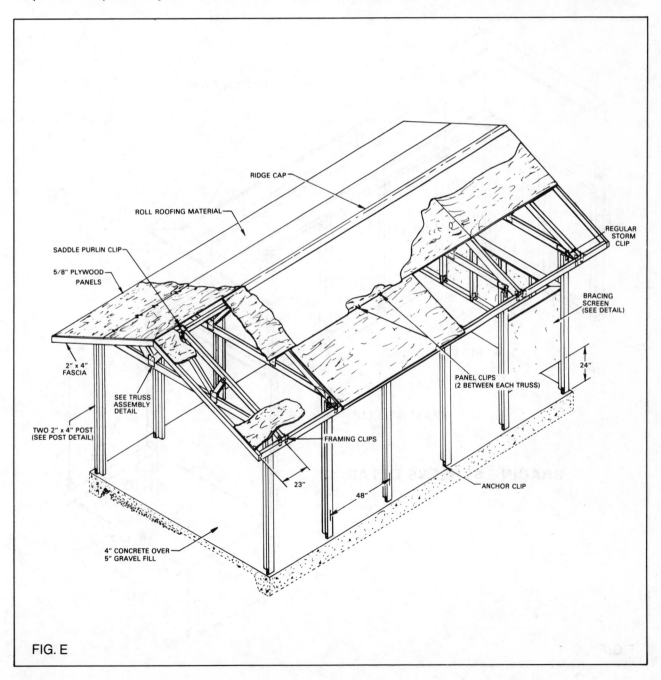

FIG. E

desired, either wood or asphalt shingles can be added as a final touch on the roof.

Applying the Bracing Screens

At this point it is best to attach the bracing screens at the rear of the carport (Fig. F). This should be built in three sections. The 2 x 3-inch framing is put together first, using Panel-Clip Framing Clips. Then, the 1/4-inch plywood sections are nailed in place. Finally, the three pieces of the 1 x 6-inch cedar cap are attached to their respective sections. Be sure to cut the miters at the corners very carefully to ensure a good fit. Nail the rear frame between the back two roof posts; then put the two side sections between the last pair of posts on each side. The bottoms of the bracing screens should be 24-inches off of the floor.

Finishing Your Carport

Your carport can be painted or finished to your taste. If desired, shingles can be added for additional water-proofing. Also, consider ways of landscaping around the carport to fully integrate its presence into your yard.

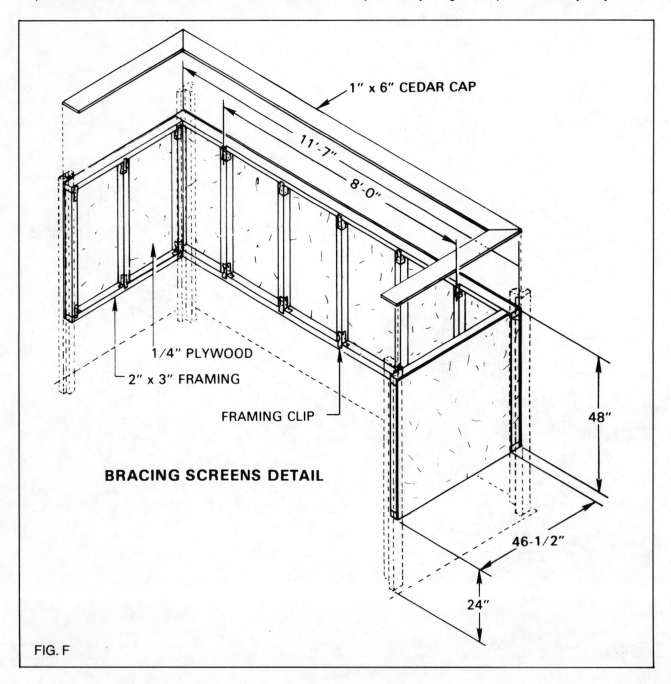

1" x 6" CEDAR CAP

11'-7"

8'-0"

1/4" PLYWOOD

2" x 3" FRAMING

FRAMING CLIP

BRACING SCREENS DETAIL

48"

46-1/2"

24"

FIG. F

LITTLE RED BARN 8′x12′ (2.4x3.6 meters)

Storage space for outdoor equipment is almost always at a premium. The little red barn solves that problem and is economical as well as attractive. It requires only an 8-foot x 12-foot (2.4x3.6 meters) site and has a spacious entrance through which you can drive a mower or small tractor. The gambrel roof adds even more storage space, allowing you to put every cubic inch of this shelter to use. (Plans courtesy of The Panel Clip Co.)

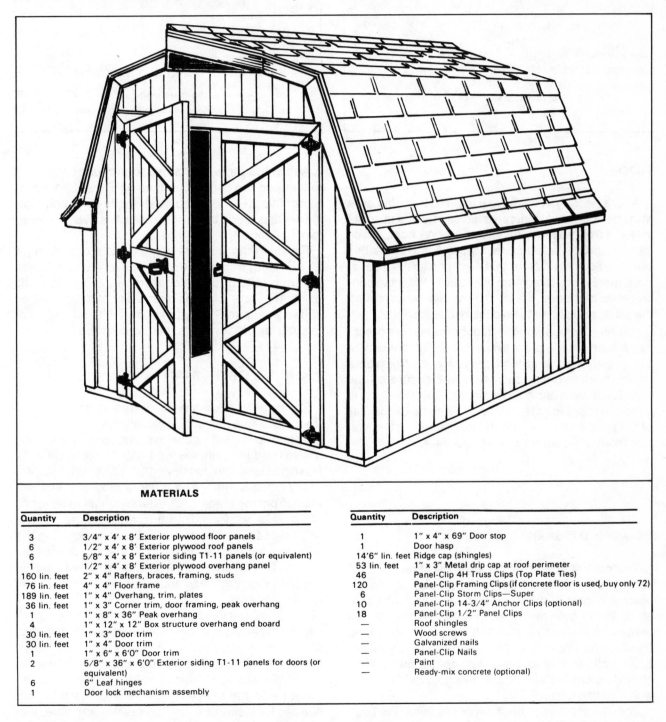

MATERIALS

Quantity	Description
3	3/4″ x 4′ x 8′ Exterior plywood floor panels
6	1/2″ x 4′ x 8′ Exterior plywood roof panels
6	5/8″ x 4′ x 8′ Exterior siding T1-11 panels (or equivalent)
1	1/2″ x 4′ x 8′ Exterior plywood overhang panel
160 lin. feet	2″ x 4″ Rafters, braces, framing, studs
76 lin. feet	4″ x 4″ Floor frame
189 lin. feet	1″ x 4″ Overhang, trim, plates
36 lin. feet	1″ x 3″ Corner trim, door framing, peak overhang
1	1″ x 8″ x 36″ Peak overhang
4	1″ x 12″ x 12″ Box structure overhang end board
30 lin. feet	1″ x 3″ Door trim
30 lin. feet	1″ x 4″ Door trim
1	1″ x 6″ x 6′0″ Door trim
2	5/8″ x 36″ x 6′0″ Exterior siding T1-11 panels for doors (or equivalent)
6	6″ Leaf hinges
1	Door lock mechanism assembly

Quantity	Description
1	1″ x 4″ x 69″ Door stop
1	Door hasp
14′6″ lin. feet	Ridge cap (shingles)
53 lin. feet	1″ x 3″ Metal drip cap at roof perimeter
46	Panel-Clip 4H Truss Clips (Top Plate Ties)
120	Panel-Clip Framing Clips (if concrete floor is used, buy only 72)
6	Panel-Clip Storm Clips—Super
10	Panel-Clip 14-3/4″ Anchor Clips (optional)
18	Panel-Clip 1/2″ Panel Clips
—	Roof shingles
—	Wood screws
—	Galvanized nails
—	Panel-Clip Nails
—	Paint
—	Ready-mix concrete (optional)

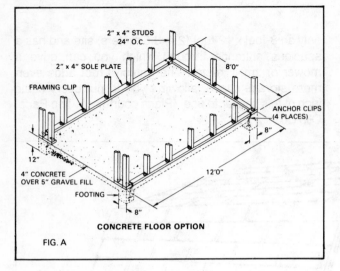

FIG. A

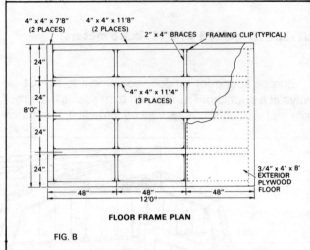

FIG. B

FLOOR

After selecting a site for your little red barn, the area must be leveled. A concrete slab can be laid in areas that are free from the danger of ground frost, which can lift and crack concrete. Figure A illustrates this optional floor plan. Note that Anchor Clips are set in the concrete at a maximum of 8' apart. When the concrete has hardened, the arms of the clips wrap around the sill or sole plates to hold them in place.

In many cases a wooden floor frame is more practical. A frame made of pressure-treated lumber can be set directly on the ground or on a bed of gravel; a gravel base is better because it will ensure a firm, level foundation and good drainage. Refer to Fig. B to assemble this type of frame using Framing Clips on all of the joints. After the frame is positioned on the site, nail down three exterior plywood panels.

FRAMING THE BARN

The next step is to frame up the entire barn. As shown in Fig. C, nail the 1" x 4" sole plate along the sides and rear of the plywood floor. Attach the side studs to the sole plates with Framing Clips, 24" on center. Then attach a 1" x 4" top plate on the studs, again using Framing Clips. The rear wall studs will extend all the way to the upper roof sections. They should be braced with 2" x 4" blocking held in place with Framing Clips.

The framing pieces for the roof are cut to the pitch shown in Fig. E using a carpenter's square. Fasten them together with Truss Clips on both sides of each joint.

Attach the three rear studs to the rear upper roof rafters and the center beam using Panel-Clip Super Storm Clips (Fig. E). Also, to strengthen the end roofing section, place three 4H Truss Clips over the rafter joints as shown.

Finishing the front framing consists of building a 2" x 4" door frame. Form a three-way joint between the front rafters, upper door frame, and front studs using 4H Truss Clips on both sides of each joint, as shown in Figure F. Also, use the 4H Truss Clip over the outside of the rafter joints, as described above.

THE FRONT OF THE BARN

The basic frame complete, turn your attention to the front of the little red barn, including the doors (Fig. G). First nail up the 5/8" exterior siding on both sides and above the door. Trim the front with 1" x 4"'s cut to fit. Next, frame up the door using 1" x 3"'s. Now you are ready to assemble the barn doors. Note that they are made from the same 5/8" exterior siding used for all of the walls, reinforced by horizontally placed 1" x 6"'s and angled 1" x 4"'s, with 1" x 3"'s running along the side and top edges, and 1" x 4"'s along the bottom edges. This door design, in particular, gives the little red barn the sturdiness and rustic look typical of old-fashioned barns.

A hasp can be fixed onto the front of the door, allowing you to secure the barn with a padlock. On the back of one side of the door you can also fasten a 1" x 4" door step for mounting additional door lock mechanisms. Details are shown in Figs. H and I. Adding these helps you to keep one door shut when it is not needed for clearance, and makes it much more difficult for intruders to force the doors apart. After fastening three hinges to each side, raise the completed doors and nail the hinges to the 1" x 3" door framing.

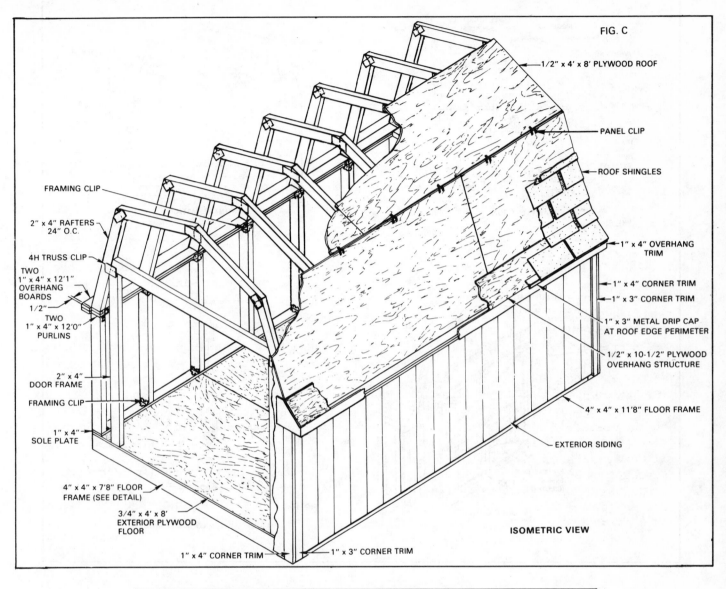

FIG. C

1/2" x 4' x 8' PLYWOOD ROOF

PANEL CLIP

ROOF SHINGLES

1" x 4" OVERHANG TRIM

1" x 4" CORNER TRIM

1" x 3" CORNER TRIM

1" x 3" METAL DRIP CAP AT ROOF EDGE PERIMETER

1/2" x 10-1/2" PLYWOOD OVERHANG STRUCTURE

4" x 4" x 11'8" FLOOR FRAME

EXTERIOR SIDING

FRAMING CLIP

2" x 4" RAFTERS 24" O.C.

4H TRUSS CLIP

TWO 1" x 4" x 12'1" OVERHANG BOARDS

1/2"

TWO 1" x 4" x 12'0" PURLINS

2" x 4" DOOR FRAME

FRAMING CLIP

1" x 4" SOLE PLATE

4" x 4" x 7'8" FLOOR FRAME (SEE DETAIL)

3/4" x 4' x 8' EXTERIOR PLYWOOD FLOOR

1" x 4" CORNER TRIM

1" x 3" CORNER TRIM

ISOMETRIC VIEW

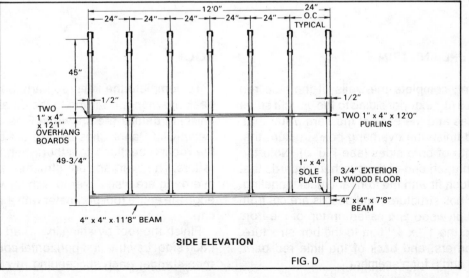

12'0"

24" O.C. TYPICAL

24" 24" 24" 24" 24" 24"

45"

1/2"

1/2"

TWO 1" x 4" x 12'1" OVERHANG BOARDS

TWO 1" x 4" x 12'0" PURLINS

49-3/4"

1" x 4" SOLE PLATE

3/4" EXTERIOR PLYWOOD FLOOR

4" x 4" x 7'8" BEAM

4" x 4" x 11'8" BEAM

SIDE ELEVATION

FIG. D

117

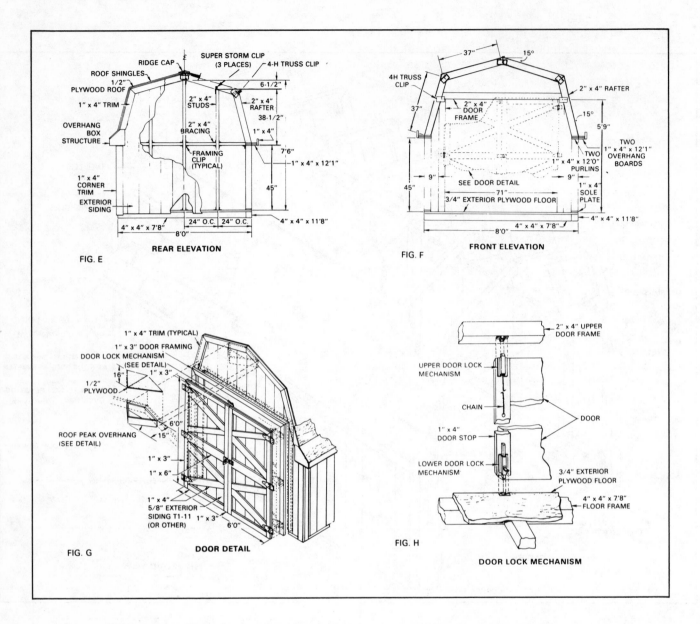

FIG. E — REAR ELEVATION

FIG. F — FRONT ELEVATION

FIG. G — DOOR DETAIL

FIG. H — DOOR LOCK MECHANISM

BOX STRUCTURE AND TRIM

At this point, complete the walls of the little red barn. Nail the 5/8'' exterior siding to the upright studs along the sides and the back of the barn. After that, frame up and finish the overhang box structure that runs the length of both sides (see Fig. J). Note the extra 1/2'' on each end of the overhang boards that allows for a flush fit with the front and back paneling. Note the four box structures end boards are cut from 5/8'' exterior plywood and nailed on top of the front paneling. Add the 1'' x 4'' trim to the box structure, the sides, corners, and back of the little red barn, using Figs. C and E for placement.

ROOF

To complete the little red barn, build the front roof peak overhang, referring to the detail in Fig. K. Roof finishing details are shown in Figs. C and G. Using Panel-Clip Panel Clips bent to the correct angle, fit the roofing sections together; then nail them to the rafters. The overhang box structure and the roof peak overhang are also covered with plywood. Be sure to edge the entire roof perimeter with a 1'' x 3'' metal drip cap.

Finish the roof by shingling. Start at the bottom of each side. Lay the first horizontal course of shingles, then stagger each succeeding row as you move up towards the peak. If the shingles are properly over-lapped, you will virtually eliminate leakage problems. When all four roof sections and the roof peak over-hang have been shingled, lay one course of shingles across the peak of the roof to act as a ridge cap.

FINISHING DETAILS

Although the little red barn can be painted the tradi-tional red and white, more unusual color combina-tions, such as green and white, white with red trim, or even a light brown stain with dark brown trim, can create interesting effects. The barn can be adapted to almost any setting. With a little landscaping and per-haps a stone walkway leading to the structure, you can easily incorporate your barn into its new sur-roundings, making for a better looking yard — and putting the car back in the garage where it belongs.

If desired, the little red barn could easily be changed into a sturdy playhouse. Replace the double door with a single one and install a small window, and we are sure that your children will enjoy is as a place of their own.

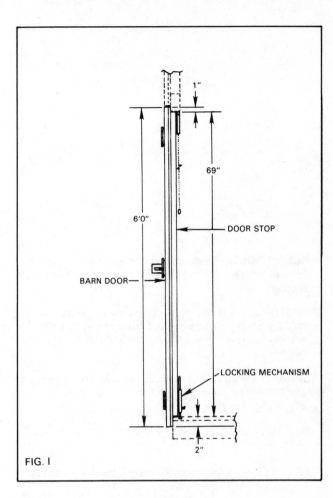

FIG. I

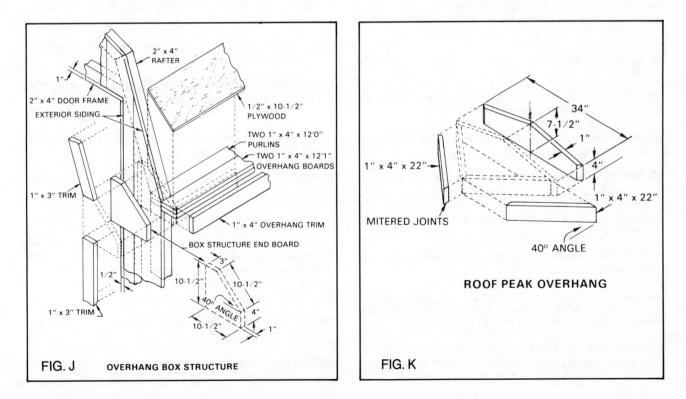

FIG. J   OVERHANG BOX STRUCTURE

ROOF PEAK OVERHANG

FIG. K

Glossary

ANCHOR BOLTS: Embedded in masonry foundation to secure framing to the foundation and prevent wind damage.

APRON: A short ramp of concrete or asphalt with a slight pitch. It is usually used from street to sidewalk and in the area immediately in front of the garage door opening.

ASPHALT: Waterproof material derived from petroleum and used for driveway paving, as well as a product used in roofing materials.

BACKFILL: Moving excavated earth back into the space adjacent to foundation walls.

BAR SUPPORT: A rigid device placed to hold reinforcing bars or fabric in the proper position before pouring concrete.

BATTEN: A thin piece of lumber used to seal or reinforce a joint.

BATTER BOARDS: Horizontal boards paired at building corners for foundation grade and alignment.

BEARING WALL: A wall that carries the load of the roof structure.

BEVELED SIDING: Horizontal strip material with bottom edge lapping top edge of the strip below.

BITUMEN: Various mixtures of hydrocarbons, such as asphalt or tar.

BLOCK: A concrete masonry unit, usually containing hollow cores.

BLOCKING: Small wood pieces used to brace framing members, provide a base for sheet materials, or a fire-stop nailed part way up a wall, between studs.

BRACE: Framing lumber placed in an inclining position to stiffen the structure; most often used as temporary bracing on walls until framing is completed.

BROOM FINISH: The surface texture resulting from stroking a broom over freshly poured concrete.

BUILT-UP ROOFING: Hot asphalt and gravel applied on roofing underlay for flat or low pitched roofs.

CANTILEVER: Floor or structure extending outward beyond vertical supports.

CAST-IN-PLACE: Mortar or concrete deposited in the place where it must harden as part of the structure. (As opposed to precast concrete.)

CHALK LINE: Mason's cord saturated with fine chalk dust for use in making line marks.

CIRCUIT: Electric wiring from current source to the point of use and back.

CIRCUIT BREAKERS: Switch-like devices that protect circuits from overload.

CODE, BUILDING: Legal restrictions by a municipality or other government agency regarding construction methods and materials.

CONCRETE: Hard-setting material made from Portland cement with sand, gravel, and water.

CONDUIT: A metal tubing system for encasing electrical wires.

CONTROL JOINT: Formed, sawed, or tooled groove in a concrete slab or structure that regulates the location and amount of cracking and separation due to dimensional change of different parts of the structure. Avoids the development of high stresses.

COURSE: Horizontal row of shingles, siding or masonry.

CRIPPLE: Framing members that are less than full length. For example, over or under a window.

CURRING: Keeping the concrete surface moist for an initial period.

DOUBLE-HUNG WINDOW: Two vertical sliding sash which bypass each other in a single frame.

DOWNSPOUT: Drain pipe on exterior wall to carry roof water from gutters to ground.

DRYWALL: Common term for gypsum wallboard, in contrast to wet-applied plaster.

EAVE: Lowest projection of a roof overhang.

ELEVATION: Drawing that shows a straight-on view.

EXCAVATING: Digging into ground for foundations.

EXPANSION JOINTS: Also called isolation joints. Separations between adjoining parts of a concrete structure, provided to allow small relative movements (such as those caused by thermal change) to occur independent of each other without serious damage.

EXPOSED-AGGREGATE FINISH: A decorative finish for concrete work achieved by removing the outer skin of mortar and exposing the coarse aggregate. This is generally done before the concrete has fully hardened.

FASCIA: Roof edge facing board nailed to rafter tails.

FIBERBOARD: Medium-density building board made from wood or vegetable fibers having some insulative properties.

FLANGES: Protruding pieces on beams, added for strength or used for attachment.

FLASHING: Metal or composition material that diverts or protects construction from moisture.

FLITCH PLATE: A thin strip of steel or other strong material inserted between two planks to strengthen them; usually a metal plate sandwiched between members and bolted together.

FLOATING: Initial leveling of a concrete surface to bring it to a coarse finish.

FOOTING: Flat, thick concrete slab serving as a base for foundation wall.

FORM WORK: Total system of support for freshly placed concrete including supporting members, hardware and necessary bracing.

FOUNDATION WALL: Bearing wall of concrete, masonry or wood for supporting first or ground floor.

FRAMING: Structural wood skeleton and supplements.

GABLE END: Triangular-shaped exterior wall immediately below edges of a gable roof. Frequently a space for application of a roof vent.

GABLE RAFTERS: Paired end rafters of a gable roof.

GAMBREL ROOF: A gable roof having two slopes per side; shallow-pitched upper slopes and steep-pitched lower slopes.

GRADING: Scraping and shifting the ground surface around a home's exterior.

GROUND FAULT INTERRUPTOR (GFI): Shock-protective device for wet-area or outdoor electrical circuits or outlets.

GROUNDING: Connecting an electrical system to earth.

GUSSET: A wood or plywood flat piece which serves as a connection at the intersection of wood members, usually trusses. The material can be fastened with nails, screws or adhesive and fastening devices.

GUTTERS: Metal or plastic troughs along roof edges for collecting roof water.

GYPSUMBOARD: Sheet material with gypsum core between two paper faces.

HARDBOARD: Sheet, panel or strip made of wood fibers compressed under heat to a dense board.

HEADER: Framing members that span an opening and support free ends of other members, such as above a door or window.

HIP FRAMING: To form a hipped roof having the same slope or pitch on all four sides.

HOLLOW-CORE DOOR: Lightweight door with interior air space, for interior use.

INSULATING BOARD: Insulative sheets that serve as sheathing boards.

INSULATION: Light-density material that reduces heat transmission; also the protective coating over electrical connectors.

JAMBS: Members at the sides of a door or window opening.

JOISTS: The horizontal framing members of a floor or ceiling.

LINTEL: Load-carrying member of steel or reinforced concrete that is used over masonry openings at doors and windows.

LOCKSET: Door-knob-and-latch assembly including a provision for locking the door.

LOUVER: Slanting overlapping slats of wood or metal fitted into framework for ventilating use.

MASONRY: Construction using brick, stone, concrete or clay tiles, usually done by a mason.

MORTAR: Portland cement, hydrated lime, sand and water mixed to embed masonry units.

MUD SILL: See Sill Plate.

MULLIONS: Vertical bars or moldings between window units.

O.C. (ON CENTER): Indicates the spacing of framing members.

OUTLETS: Electrical-system access points for lighting or appliance use.

OVERHANG: Outward projecting eave-soffit area of a roof.

PANELS: Either individual sheets or a flat assembly of parts, such as a stud wall.

PARTICLEBOARD: Sheet materials made from compressed wood chips, flakes or small particles.

PITCH: Angle or slope of a roof, slope of a pipe, and a common name for roofing bitumen.

PLATES: This tops one or two framing members running horizontally atop a wall; also the single plate on which studs rest.

PLOT PLAN: Drawings of the home and garage site or lot showing placement of the house, garage and other details.

PLUMB: Straight up and down, measured with a level.

POLYETHYLENE: Plastic ingredient for clear weatherproof film material used as a protective covering or as a vapor barrier.

PREHUNG DOORS: Door-and-frame assemblies, with the thresholds in place. The doors are sometimes prefinished.

RAFTERS: Framing members that support the roof.

RAKE: Sloping edge of a roof often trimmed with a rake board matching the eave fascia.

READY-MIXED CONCRETE: Concrete manufactured elsewhere for delivery to the purchaser while in a plastic, unhardened state.

RECEPTACLES: Electrical term for box-mounted devices that receive plug-in cords.

REINFORCING: Steel rods or metal fabric placed in concrete slabs, footings and foundations to increase their strength.

REVERSE BATTEN: A type of plywood siding in which wide boards are placed alternately over narrow boards; also a name for plywood and hardboard siding types that simulate the look.

RIDGE BOARD: Located between upper ends or rafter pairs to frame the ridge of the roof.

ROOF DECKING: Sheets or boards for sheathing over rafters.

ROOFING FELT: Building paper infused with asphalt and used as a roofing underlay.

ROLL ROOFING: Asphalt material supplied in rolls rather than in shingle form.

ROUGH OPENING: Opening in building frame for windows and doors.

SCREED: Horizontal wood or steel member staked to ground to provide a guide for top surfacing of concrete slab.

SETBACK: Minimum distance a municipality requires from the front of a home to the front property line.

SHEATHING: Boards or sheets applied over framing members to brace them and serve as a base for applying roofing and siding materials.

SILL PLATE: Bottom horizontal member of an exterior wall frame which rests atop the foundation. Sometimes called a mud sill; also sole plate, the bottom member of an interior wall frame.

SKYLIGHTS: Windows or glazed openings in roofs to provide daylight and sometimes ventilation.

SLAB: Horizontal concrete, such as a floor or drive.

SOFFIT: Underside of a roof overhang.

SPLASH BLOCK: Small masonry block placed close to the ground to receive downspout water drainage and carry it away from the building.

SQUARE: A roofing measurement term signifying 100 square feet (9.2 square meters) of area.

STARTER STRIP: Strip of prepararatory material in the first course of roofing or siding.

STORM WINDOW: An extra window usually placed on the outside of the regular window during exceptionally cold weather.

STRIATE: A narrow line or band.

STUCCO: A Portland cement plaster used for garage and house exteriors. Applied with a trowel.

STUDS: Vertical framing members of a wall.

TAPE-CEMENT JOINTS: Joint treatment for drywall panels.

THREE-WAY SWITCH: A method to control light from two locations.

THRESHOLD: Sill or bottom part of a doorway.

TOENAIL: Nailing through one member at an angle and into another.

TONGUE-AND-GROOVE: Joint treatment where one strip or sheet edge fits into edge of another. With wood boards, called Dressed-and-Matched.

TOP PLATE: Upper horizontal member in a framed wall.

TRIM: Wood, plastic or metal finishing strips.

TROWELING: Final smoothing finish for concrete.

VALLEY FRAMING: Forming an angle between two inclined roof planes.

VAPOR BARRIER: Sheet of material to stop the passage of moisture vapor.

VENTILATORS: Air exhaust or intake passage devices.

WALL ASSEMBLIES: Components for wood-frame wall construction.

WALL JACK: A pole-and-pulley assembly using rope to raise a section of wall too heavy to be lifted in place by hand.

WALL PLATE: Upper and lower horizontal members of a wall frame; also the finish cover for an electrical switch or outlet.

WATT: Electrical unit which measures the amount of current used by electrical equipment.

WEATHERSTRIPPING: Narrow strips of wood, plastic, or fiber to stop air flow at doors and windows.

WORKING DRAWINGS: Final drawings to show how a garage should be erected.

Manufacturer's List

ABL Associates
1975 E. 65th St.
Cleveland, OH 44103

Alcan Building Products
Box 511
Warren, OH 44482

Alliance Manufacturing Co.
22790 Lake Park Blvd.
Alliance, OH 44601

American Marketing Corp.
14675 Grover St.
Omaha, NE 68144

American Plywood Association
Box 11700
Tacoma, WA 98411

Arrow Group Industries
230 Fifth Ave.
New York, NY 10001

Automatic Doorman, Inc.
186 Gould Ave.
Paterson, NJ 07503

Barry Bekus Associates
8430 Santa Monica Blvd.
Los Angeles, CA 90069

California Redwood Association
1 Lombard St.
San Francisco, CA 94111

Clopay, Overhead Door Products Div.
Clopay Square
Cincinnati, OH 45214

H.W. Crane Co.
15 N. 9th Ave.
Maywood, IL 60153

Door Products, Inc.
Box 584
Bensenville, IL 60106

Frantz Manufacturing Co.
301 W. 3rd St.
Sterling, IL 61081

General Electric
Nela Park
Cleveland, OH 44112

Home Planners, Inc.
23761 Research Dr.
Farmington Hills, MI 48024

Jer Manufacturing, Inc.
Coopersville, MI 49407

Johns-Manville Sales Co.
Greenwood Plaza
Denver, CO 80217

Kaiser Aluminum
300 Lakeside Dr.
Oakland, CA 94604

Kinnear Overhead Doors
Box 216
Centralia, WA 98531

Masonite Corp.
29 N. Wacker Dr.
Chicago, IL 60606

Motor Vehicle Manufacturers Association
300 New Center Building
Detroit, MI 48202

Nutone Div., Scovill
Madison & Redbanks Rds.
Cincinnati, OH 45227

Owens-Corning-Fiberglas Corp.
Fiberglas Tower
Toledo, OH 43659

Panel Clip Co.
Box 423
Farmington, MI 48024

Portland Cement Association
5420 Old Orchard Rd.
Skokie, IL 60076

Reynolds Aluminum
Richmond, VA 23261

Ridge Doors
New Road
Monmouth Jct., NJ 08852

Shopsmith
750 Center Dr.
Vandalia, OH 45377

Stanley Door System Div.
2400 E. Lincoln Rd.
Birmingham, MI 48012

Stanley Works, Hardware Div.
New Britain, CT 06050

Stephenson Co.
Conneaut, OH 44030

Taylor Building Products
19800 Fitzpatrick
Detroit, MI 48228

Thermwell Products Co., Inc.
150 E. 7th St.
Paterson, NJ 07524

U.S. Gypsum Co.
101 S. Wacker Dr.
Chicago, IL 60606

University of Illinois, Small Homes Council
1 E. St. Mary's Rd.
Champaign, IL 61820

Jim Walter Co.
1500 N. Dale Mabry
Tampa, FL 33607

Western Wood Products Association
Yeon Building
Portland, OR 97204

Windsor Door Co., Div. of Ceco Corp.
5800 Scott Hamilton Dr.
Little Rock, AR 72209

Ordering Information For Plans

PLANS PROVIDED BY MANUFACTURERS (PLANS CAN BE OBTAINED FOR A SMALL FEE)

American Plywood Association
P.O. Box 11700
Tacoma, WA 98411
*(Pool side Garden Storage Shed,
Store-It-All Barn, Carport and Patio Shelter)*

Georgia-Pacific
Equitable Building
Portland, OR
(Outdoor Storage Center)

The Panel Clip Company
Box 423
24650 Crestview Court
Farmington, MI 48024
(Roof Truss Assembly and Installation)

The Stanley Works
P.O. Box 1800
New Britain, CT 06050
*(The Work Bench, The Potting Bench,
Child's Workbench, Basic Adult Bench,
Super Bench)*

Western Wood Products Association
Yeon Building
Portland, OR 97204
*(Carport: W-12-A, W-12-B, W-12-C,
Stow-It-All Plan, Stow-It-All Plan Project:
Idea No. 6
Great Ideas in Outdoor Living: Idea No. 7
Projects include:
Gazebo, Stow-It-All, The Sun Trap, Wood Works
Outside, The Post Lamp, The Sun Trellis*

PLANS PROVIDED BY STOCK PLAN COMPANIES FOR A FEE

Home Planners, Inc.
23761 Research Drive
Farmington, MI 48024
*Gable Roof; 2 Car Garage – Design #G-100
Attached Garage – Design #2610
Attached Garage – Design #2320
Attached Garage – Design #2174
Attached Garage – Design #1988
Attached Carport for 1-Story House
Design #2158
Attached Carport for 1-Story House
Design #2113
Slope Roof Carport – Design #2296
Flat Roof Carport – Design #1153
Flat Roof Carport – Design #1172
Flat Roof Carport – Design #1213*

Garlinghouse Company
2320 Kansas Ave., Box 299
Topeka, KS 66601

Heritage Homes Plan Service, Inc.
Dept. 106, Suite 307
3030 Peachtree Rd., N.W.
Atlanta, GA 30305

Home Building Plan Service
Studio 28J
2235 Northeast Sandy Blvd.
Portland, OR 97232

National Plan Service
435 West Fullerton
Elmhurst, IL 60126

Master Plan Service, Inc.
89 East Jericho Tpke.
Mineola, NY 11501

Index

Other Successful Books...

SUCCESSFUL ALTERNATE ENERGY METHODS, Ritchie. A guide to energy-efficient living—an imaginative treatment of a most timely subject. For homeowners caught between the high costs of changing to alternate sources of energy and the rapidly climbing costs of oil, gas and other fossil fuels, here are solutions or compromises. Details are given for tightening up insulation, solar heating possibilities, wood stoves and furnaces, geo-thermal heating and cooling, producing your own electricity and gas, and controlling the system. Tax credits and resale value of homes are also discussed. Illustrated. 250 pages. $8.95 Paperback.

SUCCESSFUL BATHROOMS, 2nd Edition, Schram. Is your bathroom as beautiful and functional as you want it to be? The smallest room in the house can be recreated easily and economically with the expert advice given here. This revised and updated edition includes water-saving devices, updated designs, remodeling, fixtures and fittings, lighting and more. Even budgeting to make the project economical. There is also new coverage of hot tubs and saunas, and a new color section. Let your creativity take over, and brightsn up this room so important to the family's daily routine. 128 pages. $6.95 Paperback.

FINISHING OFF, Galvin. An alternative to moving! Keep your present home, but add more space—or convert existing useless space into a usable attractive area. You can create new walls, convert attics and basements, or finish off unused areas in your home, with this book and a little time and energy. Complete instruction on do-it-yourself projects and advice for those wishing to use a contractor. Over 200 photos and illustrations. 144 pages. $6.95 Paperback.

SUCCESSFUL HOME GREENHOUSES, Scheller. If you have a home greenhouse, or have ever wished for one, here is a volume full of fresh, new ideas you'll want. From planning and building the greenhouse, to stocking and using it—every area is covered. Includes diagrams, site location, climate control, sunlight, heating and cooling. Over 200 illustrations, including color, help you visualize your plans. 136 pages. $6.95 Paperback.

SUCCESSFUL HOME ADDITIONS, Schram. Make it the home you've always wanted—add a carport, "Florida Room," guest room, sauna, bathroom and more! Do-it-yourself with detailed instructions, information on costs and choosing materials, and a glossary of terms that allow the homeowner to proceed to the lumberyard. Information on dealing with contractors is included. Over 350 photos guide the way for the home handyperson. 144 pages. $6.95 Paperback.

SUCCESSFUL HOME PLANS FOR THE 80'S—A collection of 188 *new* home plans compiled in cooperation with Home Planners, Inc. This book features a design presentation based upon exterior styling. Includes Tudor, Early Colonial, French, Spanish and Contemporary homes. Also Vacation Homes and Low/Medium Cost homes. There is something for everyone: full basements, lots of closets, formal rooms, open living (including decks, terraces, courtyards, and atriums), and plans for traditional two-story, split-level and ranch structures. Information on obtaining actual plans is included. Illustrated. 136 pages. $5.95 Paperback. $11.95 Hardcover.

SUCCESSFUL HOMEOWNER'S TOOLS, Ritchie. A "down-to-earth," comprehensive guide to tools, for the most simple task or the largest project in your home or apartment. It not only describes a multitude of tools, but also provides direct, complete and simple instructions on how to use them! This is not merely a catalog—it is a working guide to tools—informative to both the novice and the skilled handyperson. How to choose your tools, use them (instead of misusing them), when to rent, buy or borrow, joint ownership and common applications are covered. A MUST for every homeowner! Illustrated. 192 pages. $7.95. Paperback.

SUCCESSFUL HOW TO BUILD YOUR OWN HOME, 2nd Edition, Reschke. A completely revised and updated edition of our bestseller. You *can* build your own home with complete and detailed information—on financing, choosing a site and plans, step-by-step construction and finishing methods. *50* chapters and over 500 photos and diagrams enable most everyone to build the home of their dreams! Passive solar heating systems, woodburning furnaces and energy considerations make this book the most up-to-date reference of its kind. 352 pages. $9.95 Paperback.

SUCCESSFUL HOW TO CUT YOUR ENERGY BILLS, 2nd Edition, Derven & Nichols. Revised and updated to meet today's needs, this book gives expanded information on this timely subject. Covers economizing in the use of fuel and electricity for lighting and heating, and how to get maximum efficiency from appliances. Also, solar heat, fireplaces, and energy saving in purchasing, renovating, building and maintenance, plus a complete energy checklist. 132 pages. $6.95 Paperback.

IMPROVING THE OUTSIDE OF YOUR HOME, Schram. Upgrade the value of your home and reduce maintenance, while enjoying its improved appearance. Even the novice can improve house facades and natural settings with these easy-to-follow instructions. Basic information is given on the advantages or disadvantages of various materials, and for every element from curb to chimney to rear fence. Special emphasis is given to roof, siding, windows, doors, porches, decks, landscaping and outdoor living areas. Illustrated. 152 pages. $6.95 Paperback.

SUCCESSFUL LANDSCAPING, Felice. Streamline your landscaping efforts with expert advice and save yourself time and expense. This beautifully illustrated book will guide you toward a professional-looking lawn and garden. Includes sections on vegetable gardening, disease prevention and lawn maintenance, bird feeders, decks and patios. Planting schedules, glossary of terms, and chemical products are included in appendices. Your home deserves the lovely setting you can easily provide. 128 pages. $6.95 Paperback.